Daren and Nikia Hammonds-Blakely

CROSSES AND CROWNS
A Counseling Guide for Living as Champions in Marriage

CROSSES AND CROWNS
A Counseling Guide for Living as Champions in Marriage

Published by Literacy in Motion
Phoenix, Arizona
www.AnthonyThigpen.com

Anthony KaDarrell Thigpen
Editor-in-Chief

Library of Congress Cataloging-in-Publication Data Publisher and Printing by Literacy in Motion
Cover Design by Literacy in Motion Design Team

CROSSES AND CROWNS
A Counseling Guide for Living as Champions in Marriage
ISBN: 978-0-578-44749-0

Self-Help/Autobiographical
Printed in the United States of America

CROSSES AND CROWNS
Daren and Nikia Hammonds-Blakely
A Counseling Guide for Living as Champions in Marriage

Dedication & Acknowledgements

This book is an accumulation of so many years, tears & experiences that have shaped our marriage over the past decade. We never could have imagined making it to this season without God. Our first and fullest thanks goes to God, our father, for designing the institution of marriage and hand choosing us to experience it, together. With the help and strength of God we have faced and conquered trials we never anticipated and through it all, we have found our faith and relationship with God and each other to be stronger than ever before. We'd also like to thank our parents and grandparents for giving us an invaluable foundation and source of impartation: The late Bishop William O. & Mother Annie Mae Blakely, Pastor David & Mother Delores Blakely, The late Pastor Chester & Mother Floye Simmons, Pastor Rozelle & the late Mother Gladys Hammonds, Peter Hammonds & Mickey Micou.

`We would also like to acknowledge those who have given us spiritual leadership and the first trust and honor of working in marriage ministry: Pastor Larry & Natalie Dyer (Praise Fellowship Worship Center) and Bishop Joby and Pastor Sheryl Brady (The Potter's House of North Dallas). Special thanks also

Dedication and Acknowledgments continued...

goes to our spiritual advisors, counselors and accountability partners, the late Pastor Eugene Banks, Apostle Sean Anike and Pastors Jason and Chaquita Anglin. While we are blessed with many supportive friends and family members, special thanks go to a couple of our closest friends and confidants: Gregory and Tia Airrington and Willie & Jermeka Smith. Thank you for the many years of faithful and unwavering friendship and support.

We are thankful to our children and grandchildren for their support of us and this project, from its inception to completion. Much love to our young king and queen Armani & Chanel Blakely, and our three princesses: Christian, Nicole & Naria.

Lastly, there would be no book to publish if it were not for our dear friend and brother, Anthony KaDarrell Thigpen. Just as a first-time parent can't trust just anyone with their newborn, we could never even imagine doing this project without you. You are so much more than our publisher. You are a man who has helped birth our dreams into reality. We look forward to many more years of partnership and collaboration.

Daren to Nikia:

Honey, I'm grateful for you, your love, loyalty and commitment. You are my 2nd heartbeat. I love you very much. I will never take for granted your undying love for our family and the children. From day one, you have been "all in". We have grown laughed, cried and grown together and I can't imagine a life without you in it. -Love, DB

Nikia to Daren:

Babe, you truly are the love of my life. I'm so grateful to you for showing me a love that I've never known or experienced. Your unconditional love and faithfulness has strengthened and blessed me. I'm eternally thankful for you and look forward to many more years in love and in life as Mrs. Blakely. - Love, Lubi

Table of Content

Introduction/p. 11-14
The Reality is...

Chapter 1/p. 15-24
Rebounding from Infidelity

Chapter 2/p. 25-32
Life After Divorce

Chapter 3/ p. 33-41
Facing Infertility

Chapter 4/p. 42-49
Re-Marriage:
Letting Go of the Past, Planning for The Future

Chapter 5/p. 50-61
Sex and Intimacy

Chapter 6/p. 62-72
Building Core Commonalities

Chapter 7/p. 73-81
Blended Family:
Step-Parenting, Raising Somebody Else's Child

Chapter 8/p. 82-89
In Sickness and in Health

Chapter 9/p. 90-95
The Case for Counseling

Chapter 10/p. 96-103
Building Your Inner Circle

Chapter 11/p. 104-114
Personality Differences and Communication Styles

Chapter 12/p. 115-122
I Changed My Mind:
Spouse Changes Sexuality, Identity and Preferences

Chapter 13/p. 123-132
Overcoming Loss:
Repossession and Foreclosure

Chapter 14/p. 133- 139
Dealing with Death:
How to Keep Grief from Killing the Marriage

CROSSES & CROWNS

Introduction
THE REALITY IS...

I In a time where reality TV and social media popularity are at an all-time high, it is easy to get caught up in the images we see of others. Somehow the mind vicariously compares our own realities with theirs. Some of us are trying to *Keep Up with the Kardashians* while others are trying to live the lifestyle of *Real Housewives*. Many of the images we see on television and internet sources like Facebook, Instagram and Snapchat are in most cases, exaggerated highlight reels of people's lives. Our routine life and everyday marriage takes place behind the scenes. If we could take a closer look at people's lives behind closed doors and without the cameras and facades, we might be shocked at the realities we see. We may even look at our own lives and realize that rather than wishing we had theirs, we'd be more grateful for our own.

The truth is, we can't compare our marriages to others. We each have our own formula. The chemistry and criteria that makes your marriage work is not necessarily the ingredients for others. Celebrate what you have. The components that work for some marriages, might destroy others. The best thing we can do to ensure the long-term survival and vitality of our marriage is be honest, present and committed to our own unique union. We must first be honest because marriage can't work if we are pretending to be someone we are not. Our spouse has to be able to see, honor and accept us for who we are. We must also be willing to do the same for them. After facing and accepting who we are, we have to then be fully present. This means bringing our full self to the table, every day and in every way. We can't afford to check out on our spouses. If our jobs, churches and families can demand so much from us, certainly our spouses deserve our full attention. Moreover, we must remain committed. Our vows will be forced to withstand the test of time – in every imaginable way. There will be days when we don't feel like keeping the promises we've made. We must be committed to making the daily choice to say "I DO" over and over again. Marriage is a daily choice to be present, submit and commit ourselves to each other.

Marriage can get complicated. Honoring husbands as kings and celebrating wives as queens comes with unforeseen challenges. Happily-ever-after ends with divorce for about 50% of marriages. Many couples reject counseling as taboo. Crosses and Crowns is an intimate resource guide for couples with reservations about traditional counseling.

There are no experts on marriage. We are each walking this journey daily. Throughout this book we tried to use words like "us" and "we" because we want readers to know they you are not alone. No matter where you are in your marriage, others have been there as well. Hopefully, this book will help us all build the kind of marriages we've always wanted. We deserve our happily-ever-after. We did not write this book as the authority on issues revolving around marriage, we are merely participants.

In time, honesty, communication, commitment and forgiveness will cause our marriage relationship to grow deeper in love. God created this great institution. He has great plans to prosper it and maximize the potential of what it can become. Stay the course. Through better *and* worse, through richer *and* poorer, and through sickness *and* health, we can each find the love and hope our marriage needs to thrive. It won't be easy, but it will definitely be worth it. Remember, we must bear our crosses in order to wear our crowns!

Wishing you success in life and in marriage,
Daren & Nikia

Chapter 1
REBOUNDING FROM INFIDELITY

Most people dream about their happily ever after, especially females. As children we create images of what we want our lives to look like as adults. Whether we start with our Barbie and Ken fantasies, or teddy bear wedding parties, many of us begin picturing our weddings early. We visualize the perfect wedding day followed by a romantic and adventurous honeymoon. We envision our flawless life with our perfect spouse. Every girl wants a wedding with a princess tiara (crown) and every boy aspires to be the king of his castle. Hence, the concept, crosses and crown. With those images embedded in our minds, we lead our lives and pursue our partners, hoping for the best - and expecting it. Then life happens. We realize that the weight of our crosses come with the honor of crowns. We find ourselves in committed relationships hoping that our partner shares mutual feelings toward us and marriage. Unfortunately, for many, our hopes of happily-ever-after are burned to ashes from the consuming sensation of infidelity. Infidelity ignites a burning breach of trust that is difficult to extinguish. Visions of our future do not include painful scenarios of affairs. Our childhood visions don't factor an equation of a future spouse obliterating our love, intimacy, trust and security. Child-like aspirations don't adequately prepare us for adult challenges. Infidelity is a tragedy that causes torment and tears when our spouse disrespects what we consider sacred. It requires a higher level of maturity to cope with bedroom affairs. Without question, infidelity can be one of the most painful, humiliating and debilitating experiences one could ever have - especially if you're genuinely blind-sighted.

Being blind-sighted is devastating. Inevitably, being confronted with evidence of an affair can be very damaging to our psyche. After exhibiting dedication, determination, and duty, having a spouse secretly sneak in extramarital affairs is disturbing, to say the least. So much so, that it often hurts our future ability to fully trust. When individuals devote their entire life to one person who proves capable of living an alternative existence, our reality shifts. Infidelity can not only shatter our faith in marriage, it can also shake our faith in God, people and even ourselves.

Don't blame yourself. While this is almost an instinctive reaction, the fact is, it is the very nature of love to "Hope all things," "Bear all things" and "Believe all things." Love hides a multitude of faults, according to I Corinthians 13. Love covers. That's a wonderful thing when you think about Christ's love for his children. Love can simultaneously be a gift and a challenge. In essence, love blindly overlook faults. It's not that we intend to be oblivious, it's just that once we're involved, it's harder to see our situation objectively. Different dynamics dictate our perspectives. It's similar to observing a loving mother interact with her disruptive child. While onlookers see an obnoxious child in need of discipline, some mothers subjectively see such behavior as cute. Love adores what others call irritating. Love makes us see hope where there is despair. That same love often causes us to ignore warning signs. It's not because we're stupid. It's because we're in love. Don't blame yourself. Not seeing, expecting or preparing for the devastation of infidelity and other broken promises, doesn't mean we were unwise. We were just believing in our happily-ever-after. Everyone deserves it, but not many of us will get it. Recent studies from the American Psychological Association reveal that up to 50-percent of married couples in the United States end in divorce. The divorce rate for subsequent marriages is even higher. Surprisingly, Christian divorce rates are only 38%, based on multiples studies completed as recent as 2015. We will explore why when discussing *Building Core Commonalities*. How we choose to deal with these staggering realities will define the outcome of our marriage. Our perspective also prepares us for each step forward into our new season.

It's time to face the music without getting bitter – choose to get better. Confrontation after the discovery of infidelity and broken trust is a logical next step. How we address this delicate matter is important and consequence-bearing.

The 1995 movie, *Waiting to Exhale*, highlights a heart-wrenching exposure of an extramarital affair. Her husband of 11-years, father of her two children, abandoned the marriage upon having an affair with a white co-worker. The role of Bernadine Harris, played by Angela Bassett, cleared her husband's closet and burned everything in his car. He banned her from the company she helped him to build. Through the eyes of these characters, we saw many of the *Do's and Don'ts* of marital hurt, confrontation and recovery. For example, *don't* take your spouse's clothes and create a bonfire on the property of your home. *Don't* solicit the children and conduct a yard sale of your spouse's possessions and seemingly "meaningless" family mementos. On the other hand, *do* solicit advice from a trusted source, pastor, or network of like-minded friends. *Do* consider making steps to re-create a future with your desires and hopes for a better outcome. Most importantly, if you're contemplating cheating on your spouse, *don't.* Bernadine decided to go for a new sassy haircut - one that she had always wanted, but never followed up on due to her spouse's wishes. At the end of the day, unlike Bernadine, we must pray and meditate. We must seek wisdom and grace to proceed through this painful experience. Pray for peace. When men and women go through the challenges of infidelity, either you will become bitter or better – the end result depends on how you handle it. Prayer and meditation empowers us to come through in a manner that won't jeopardize years of our personal progress. None of us can predict exactly how we will initially react, whether with profanity, arguing or physical battery. Christians should aim to come through this trial in a way that pleases Christ. We should seek mature strategies, escape criminal activity, and avoid the evening news.

Expect denials and excuses. It would be ideal for unfaithful spouses to confess when confronted. Own it. Repent. Forsake it. It just doesn't typically happen that way. Have you ever caught a child sneaking in the cookie jar? Many times, with crumbs falling from their mouths, when caught red-handed, they say, "I'm not doing anything". Denial is a common response. In a 2005 article in Psychology Today, Dr. Saul Levine explored how humans often will deny reality, even if there is scientific proof to tell us otherwise. Even more revealing was a study by his colleague, Dr. Carl Alasko, in the same publication who looked at why people's first instinct is to make excuses and shift blame. Alasko said, "Because humans experience a range of powerful and complex emotions, such as desire, greed, pride, revenge, need for status, shame, humiliation, etc., these emotions exert a strong influence over a person's ability to interpret facts."

Regardless of whether the root cause of our tendencies toward denial are nature versus nurture, just know that denial and blame-shifting is normal when confronting infidelity. Infidelity is an emotional issue, but we can't afford to address it emotionally. As we've discussed earlier, our hearts can be deceitful (see Jeremiah 17:9-10) and misleading because of it's design to cover faults. So, when confronting infidelity, let the facts outmaneuver feelings and proceed with wisdom, caution and counseling.

Forgive. Do it completely and quickly. When our hearts are broken and our trust is abused, the last thing on our mind is forgiveness. Yet, forgiveness is most necessary. Forgiveness is the consequential thing in our process of confrontation, healing and recovery from infidelity. It's wisely said that forgiveness is not for the villain, it's the secret ingredient that transforms the victim into the victor. Truer words have never been spoken. Forgiveness of infidelity and breached trust does not necessarily mean reconciliation. It is the act of letting go of the resentment and need for revenge. Long-lasting feelings of unforgiveness have both spiritual and natural effects. For those of us who are Christians, we are taught we should forgive, because we are forgiven. Forgiveness is a difficult reality for Christians and Non-Christians, alike. Matthew 6:14-15 explains, *"For if you forgive other people when they sin against you, your heavenly Father will also forgive you. But if you do not forgive others their sins, your Father will not forgive your sins."* Forgiveness, or the lack thereof, is sure to produce natural and physical ramifications. Medical research from the world-renowned Mayo Clinic cited, "Letting go of grudges and bitterness can make way for improved health and peace of mind." According to studies and research conducted by the Mayo Clinic, they conclude forgiveness can lead to:

- Healthier relationships
- Improved mental health
- Less anxiety, stress and hostility
- Lower blood pressure
- Fewer symptoms of depression
- A stronger immune system
- Improved heart health
- Improved self-esteem

If we ever expect to experience our happily-ever-after, it starts within. Making the kind of choices to be proactive about our spiritual and emotional wellness. Our life is a gift intended to be enjoyed. However, we will never enjoy anything until we realize that joy comes from within. Forgiveness is our cure to prevent people from poisoning our happily-ever-after.

CHAMPIONS IN MARRIAGE
Questions & Discussion
Chapter 1: Rebounding from Infidelity

1. Have you ever experienced someone cheating on you?

2. How did you react once you found out?

3. How did that experience impact you negatively? Positively?

_____

_____

_____

_____

_____

_____

_____

Chapter 2
LIFE AFTER DIVORCE

Life after divorce is what we make it. That may sound oversimplified, but it's true. Divorce is devastating. It is a kind of death. Whether we are the ones who filed or not, the process of divorce can often still feel like a loss, because it's a death of all the plans and dreams we had for this particular marriage.

"There is no such thing as a "broken family." Family is family, and is not determined by marriage certificates, divorce papers, and adoption documents. Families are made in the heart. The only time family becomes null is when those ties in the heart are cut. If you cut those ties, those people are not your family. If you make those ties, those people are your family. And if you hate those ties, those people will still be your family because whatever you hate will always be with you."
— C. Joybell C.

Undoubtedly, when we first exchanged rings and said vows, "until death do us part," that's exactly what we envisioned would happen. We picture ourselves with our spouse, old and gray in rocking chairs, enjoying our children and grandchildren until the end. Now, in reality many of us face the end of our marriage in just years, months, maybe less. What's worse, some of us reach significant milestones, perhaps the 10th, 25th or even 50th year anniversary, only to see our matrimony wither prematurely. Feelings of failure, hopelessness and cynicism may creep in and convince us that the way it is now is the way it will always be. Truth is, time heals heartbreak. In the moment, we may feel like we will never laugh, love or live again, but in time, we will – we absolutely will. No matter how cold and harsh winter is, it always gives way to spring. Choose to take one day at a time, and be grateful for the lessons learned in our last experience. A new season is on the horizon – things will get better. Let's choose to take one day at a time.

Learning how to be alone again will have its challenges. Anyone who tells us otherwise is delusional or hasn't been through it. There are so many simple things that can serve as triggers. Many will miss the physical presence of their spouse. The lack of having someone laying beside us, or just present in the house can initially be quite daunting. Some days it will just hurt to not have that person to come home to and bounce ideas off. It's not unusual to miss the reality of having a spouse to share daily ups and downs. Others may miss more of the non-physical things like the sound of laughter, scents or other little idiosyncrasies. We may not have fully noticed or appreciated certain aspects of our spouse until they're gone. Holidays, birthdays, vacations and special events will also be difficult. The loss of safety and the sensation of protection, disposition of children, financial support and accountability, and sharing daily responsibilities is difficult. The road will be rough. Just know that figuring out how to live life as a single person again, will take some getting used to.

Getting through family gatherings and holidays will take time and patience. Holidays and special events are times when most family gatherings take place. Even if we typically do most things alone, these occasions tend to anticipate the attendance of both spouses. During the first noticeable absence of our former spouse, it's likely to feel awkward. Christmas dinners, weddings, funerals and graduations may take on a whole new dynamic when re-acclimating to single life. The chances of feeling out of place are increased – no one likes feeling like a third wheel. There can also be an inward struggle to feel and act normal in what otherwise would have been a joyous occasion. Take Heart. Not only will a sense of normalcy eventually be restored, but many times we will discover renewed relationships with family and friends. God never leaves us comfortless. When least expected, we'll receive that phone call from an aunt encouraging us to keep going. We'll hear from a distant friend who has recently learned of our new relationship status, who genuinely reaches out to support. Sure, they'll be individuals who'll try to get the juicy details – digging for negativity. However, as we find strength to pull ourselves up, we will also find people who have walked our paths. They have insight to share and empathy to offer. They understand our pain – let those people in. There's nothing like having a listening ear or someone to pray for us. God graciously places people like that in our lives when we open our hearts and allow it. We need these people to survive. However, we must be careful not to put our entire hope and trust in them. They are not a replacement spouse, and can not fulfill our needs. Our family members and friends are humans. As much as they may love us, they too have limitations and personal lives.

Expect the loyalties of friends and family to change. One of the more painful dynamics of divorce is watching relationships change. Emotional connections with our spouses' family and mutual friends will likely deteriorate. Many married couples adopt the utopian thought of "your family is my family". We begin building and establishing relationships with our spouse's parents, siblings, relatives and children as though they are our own. We go in full-steam ahead loving and pouring into those family members, without entertaining the thought that they may one day exit our lives. That's just what divorce does – it draws a line in the sand that separates us from people that have become woven in our hearts. In cases of people who have been married 20, 30, 50 years, their families have become our family. For some family members, we may be the only uncle, aunt, mother, and/or father they know. The decision to divorce is not just hard on us, but think of the countless people that have become interwoven as a result of our unions. Beyond just our families, we now have mutual relationships with friends, co-workers, church, school and community club members, and the list goes on. While some individuals mentally prepare for the pain of shattered and separated relationships, most people fail to contemplate the other relationship dynamics that may change.

The dissolution of a union is in many ways a desecration of a well-connected community. It causes confusion, isolation, and conflict. It forces people to feel the need to take sides – and most people will. People often feel that a story needs a hero and a villain, so they will assign those roles to us and our spouses, dependent upon whom they are most influenced by. Children aren't the only ones who suffer with divided loyalties when divorce occurs, adults do too – maybe even more so. Friends and relatives who don't choose sides, aiming to stay neutral, often avoid routine communication all together. It's often times the only way they know how to stay out of it. This is a common effort to avoid appearing partial to one side over another.

Let relationships, not titles, define who our family is. We started this chapter with the quote from C. Joybell. There is so much truth in the sentiment that there doesn't have to be a such thing as a broken family. Families are made from intentionally building committed relationships. Family ties can survive the blow of divorce, distance and any other status change life may throw at us. If we are intentional about maintaining those relationships, we can. Sure, the adjustment will be awkward at first, but deep roots can not easily be plucked. It may feel like when we lose our spouse we will lose everything and everyone that came with them, but not necessarily. God has a way of preserving the relationships of people that truly love and mean us the best.

CHAMPIONS IN MARRIAGE

Questions & Discussion

Chapter 2: Life After Divorce or Long-Term Relationship

1. When it comes to the end of your marriage, did you see it coming, or did you feel blind-sighted?

2. Describe life after the break up.

3. How have you changed since then, positively? negatively?

_____

_____

_____

_____

_____

_____

Chapter 3
FACING INFERTILITY

Once you get married, the next step is babies, right? There was once a popular nursery rhyme used whenever there was a suspicion of a new crush. The rhyme went something like this:

*"Jack and Jill sitting in a tree, **K – I – S – S – I – N – G,** first comes love, then comes marriage, then comes girl [name] with a baby carriage."*

Perhaps you remember it – maybe you've even recited it. That rhyme has caused many of us to blush over the years. It's cute and innocent. The only thing is, that rhyme, along with many other reinforcements of its kind, indoctrinates children. It sends a subliminal message that normalcy requires a sequence of love, followed by marriage and ultimately a baby. It's almost like our love story isn't complete until a child comes into the picture. Think about it, movies and TV shows always feature a husband, wife and children. Even seemingly asexual TV couples like Ricky and Lucy Ricardo or Fred and Wilma Flintstone, who slept in completely different beds, still ended up pregnant. The indoctrinated message, especially for children, is that love should result in marriage, and then childbirth.

Furthermore, as Christians, we're taught to believe that one of God's main intentions and desires for us is to "be fruitful and multiply" (Genesis 1:28). From the days of Adam and Eve, we can see how God designed marriage and family. According to scripture, God takes great pleasure in both. Even God himself, not having a wife, still had a son. With all that in mind, parenting just seems like it should be a part of the package of what adults do, right? The desire for a child is so embedded within us that we don't even realize it's there – until one day we realize it's there. The desire for a child can be haunting, daunting and downright exhausting. The pressure to conceive is a real issue for many couples, both internally and externally. For most young couples, no sooner we return from our honeymoon, the next question we'll often get is "So, when are you going to have children?" The birthing and raising of children is undoubtedly one of God's most precious and rewarding gifts. For many couples, despite our *desire* to conceive, we find ourselves in a position whereas we can not. The desire for a child can be one of the most exasperating longings imaginable. One of the most famous illustrations of this sense of longing, comes from the biblical account of Hannah, in the first chapter of Samuel. Hannah was a young wife who desperately wanted a child. She cried, she begged and she prayed. One day, while in the temple crying out to the Lord, the priest Eli mistook her as a drunk. How upset and disheveled must she have been to have the appearance of being intoxicated? Her heart was waxed sore. Hannah was one of the first, but she most certainly won't be the last. Millions of women every year, suffer from infertility despite their deepest desires and greatest efforts. What's worse, is when you have to watch others birth the one thing you would give your life to have.

Celebrating the conception of others takes grace. Visualize yourself starving after days of hunger, feeling exhaustion and a cantankerous edginess. We have sporadic emotions and a short temper sparked from ravenous hunger. While sitting at a table with a friend who'd recently ate, you're desperately hoping for a meal. Your friend came for fellowship, but you needed food. Suddenly, the waitress provides a platter of your favorite foods to your friend. In that moment, how do you think you might feel? What are some of the instinctive thoughts that might come to your mind? Whatever your feelings, be assured that you're not alone. It's a natural response. We have to be intentional about celebrating others, as it might not come naturally. Being happy for someone who receives the very thing you are praying for, may not come naturally, but it is possible. Grace gives us the ability to respond to people and situations gentler, more tempered and more wisely than we would, without that little bit of divine intervention. For those of us living with the very real pains and struggles of infertility, we're not alone. According to the National Infertility Association, 1 in every 6 couples will struggle to conceive. That's over 15 million men and women each year. We must continue to pray to accept what God allows. Meanwhile, we must continue to pray to accept what God allows and be intentional about celebrating those who are blessed to conceive. This attitude will redirect resentment.

Infertility is nobody's "fault"- don't blame yourself, God or your partner. For couples trying to conceive, there can be a tendency to self-evaluate or internalize a sense of blame. While it's true that women are more commonly associated with infertility, it also effects 30-40% of all males. Regardless of biology, as Christians, we believe that all life and the ability to conceive is in the hands of God. God is superior to science and convention even in conception. According to biblical accounts, the story of Sarah, Abraham's wife, is proof of God's ability to create life. Sarah was 90 years old when she conceived her son Isaac. In fact, the very news of her eminent pregnancy made her laugh out loud. Both she and her husband Abraham were considered to be sterile and completely infertile. As sure as the Lord promised child birth, He performed it. Many women throughout the Bible share that testimony of miraculous conception. But probably most notable of all biblical conceptions, is the story of Mary, the mother of Jesus. She got pregnant without sexual intercourse or physical means. What God desires and promises will happen. It may be delayed, but it won't be denied. There are also many modern-day accounts of miraculous conceptions. A Tribune242 news article entitled, Miracle of Conception, was released in 2000. There was a husband and wife by the name of Thomas and Alexandria Darville-Sawyer who struggled over a decade with infertility. However, God gave them a promise of conception years prior. Despite many obstacles and seemingly insurmountable odds, God's will prevailed.

According to Job 1:21, "*Naked I came from my mother's womb, and naked I will depart. The Lord gave and the Lord has taken away; may the name of the Lord be praised.*" The premise behind this scripture is the power to give, sustain and take life is ultimately in the hands of God alone. Sometimes, if we are allowed to conceive a child it is easier to accept it as the will of God. However, we also have to be willing to accept God's will if we don't conceive. There are financially prosperous people, able to pay for expensive procedures, yet remain unable to conceive. If pregnancy doesn't happen for couples who desire it, it is important that we not blame ourselves, our spouses or God.

"Many are the plans in a person's heart, but it is the Lord's purpose that prevails" (Prov. 19:21).

It is well. Accepting the will of God concerning conception can be easier in theory than application. While the heart wants what the heart wants, we have to trust that God's will is best for our lives. Thus, He knows how to care for, cover and protect our hearts even more than we can. While we can't promise that all couples trying to conceive will actually conceive, we can promise that all things, even the painful occurrences throughout life, will work together for our good. Infertility may not feel good, yet our fundamental hope as Christians is that God will manifest His goodness in spite of. As a result, our lives will manifest greater blessings and opportunities handcrafted for our purpose. A recent article from Parent.com emerged an encouraging story about a couple trying to conceive:

> "After getting married in 2001, Ashley and James began trying to conceive. When we first started trying, I was obsessive and bought many pregnancy tests even if I knew my period was coming," says Ashley. "We probably spent hundreds of dollars on tests. We viewed making love as work, and it took the pleasure and

enjoyment out of it." Eventually they went to a specialist and discovered that James had a low sperm count, so the couple faced the possibility that they may never have children. "I was at the point that I didn't even want to get out of bed some days. I was so depressed," she says. One day, Ashley had a moment of clarity. "I just kept telling myself that when the time was right we would get pregnant," she says. "It's hard, and you often think that there's something wrong with you, and there really wasn't." Much to the couple's surprise, they got pregnant a few months after resigning themselves to the idea of being childless. Daughter Natalie was born in September 2003. They recently received another surprise: twins due in August, conceived without the couple even trying.

Keep The Faith! God is Able. For those of us that will not experience physical conception, God will still use us to birth innumerable blessings if we continue to believe (see Isaiah 54:1).

CHAMPIONS IN MARRIAGE
Questions & Discussion
Chapter 3: Infertility

1. How long have you desire a child?

2. How do you imagine your life, after the birth?

3. What if it conception doesn't happen, would you be able to live happily with that?

_____

_____

_____

_____

_____

_____

_____

Chapter 4
RE-MARRIAGE:
Letting Go of the Past, Planning for The Future

"I will never go through that again!" That's a common phrase following a failed marriage. After divorce, many of us feel we will never marry again. We fear never finding a person who will genuinely accept and love us. We often feel like we have just blown our one true chance at happiness. Others transition feelings of hopelessness to a sense of resolve. I will not allow myself or another person a chance to hurt me in that way again. Just as sure as God is faithful to give us second chances at salvation, dreams and desires, He often allows us second chances at happily-ever-after. The goal, however, is not to live a different life, but to intentionally and prayerfully make this life *better*. Without the proper approach, a new marriage will be a replication of the failures of the past. There must be real effort and intention to learn, grow and correct the missteps of the last relationship. Even if we feel our former spouse bears the brunt of the responsibility, there are still many lessons to be learned and healing to be had from any failed relationship.

What will be different this time? This question should be answered with support and a concerted effort to seek wise counsel. This counsel might be sought from mentors, close friends, pastors, spiritual leaders or other professionals. We often don't see ourselves the way others do. It could be of extreme benefit to hear another's perspective on decisions made and actions taken, and how they may have played a role in end results. Proverbs 12:15 says, *"The way of a fool is right in his own eyes, but a wise man listens to advice."* Likewise, clinical and therapeutic counseling is an invaluable resource. Sometimes, as Christians, we use religious jargon and clichés as crutches to avoid dealing with our demons. We have to tackle our own personal issues if we plan to live a more productive life. Christian counselors and licensed therapists can be some of our greatest allies. They offer invaluable insights and tools that have both practical and spiritual relevance. Every new storm, obstacle, or ruined relationship, offers us a new chance for making *better* choices. Most people make new choices, but not *better* ones. Becoming *better* can only happen by examining, learning, growing and healing from our past relationships.

Our new spouses deserve a clean slate. Unavoidably, we are all the sum total of our past experiences – both good and bad. They make us who we are today. We cannot forget or erase the past. However, it is our responsibility to prevent the past from effecting our new marriages. Past solutions may not be applicable in our future. Through long and healthy dialogues, counseling and introspection, we have to now present ourselves to our new spouses as emotional virgins to the marriage relationship. We may not be able to reverse our physical virginity, but we can reset our thinking, expectations and behaviors. This empowers the relationship and assures the spouse that they are experiencing the best version of ourselves. Nobody wants sloppy seconds or leftovers – neither do they want to crawl in the shadows of a previously villainized spouse. If we are not yet healed and recharged enough to over-extend ourselves to our new partner, we are not ready for remarriage. If we are going into this relationship because we somehow think it's going to be easier, we are not ready for remarriage. If we still have dreams and feelings causing us to imagine the physical presence of our past partner, we are not ready for remarriage. In fact, statistics say that while 50% of first marriages end in divorce, the rate of divorce is as high as 67% for second marriages. Third marriages have an even higher divorce rate of 74%.

The way we start is the way we finish – healthy dating will make or break a relationship. Many of us who have been in long-term marriages find it hard to get back into dating mode. Dating is something that should be approached seriously and not cavalierly. We should never play games with our hearts and minds, instead, we must guard them. After spending countless years in a relationship it's hard to re-adapt to single life. We will need a healthy support system to direct us and safeguard us from jumping into a potentially problematic relationship. Sometimes, just the need for companionship alone or the desire for physical intimacy will tempt us to jump into a new relationship prematurely. For individuals under religious influence, a famous quote is "It's better to marry than to burn". This statement implies rather than risk going to hell, get married. Guilt-driven marriages are about having authorized sex, verses love, commitment and happiness. Although sex may be one of our greatest incentives for marriage, it should be lower on the priority list. At the first thought of marriage, many of us are so enamored at the idea of an everlasting love, that we fail to count up the costs to maintaining it. We must prepare our hearts and lives for marriage. Following a failed marriage, having experienced ups and downs our outlook is usually more cautious. It is imperative that when given a do-over, we take the opportunity to truly create a priority list based on things that are most essential. That list will look differently for many of us. For some, communication and the ability to mentally connect and stimulate conversation may be at the top of list. The priority for others may be financial security and the ability to properly plan for the future. Some people may indeed make sex their priority. However, most of us will agree, the second time around, our priorities seem to evolve – perhaps because we, ourselves, have evolved. Whatever our evolution results in, it is important that we discuss it when dating. The start of the dating relationship should be marked by setting the tone and expectation of what we truly need and desire. Our expectation should be based on experiences, not wishful thinking, childhood fantasies or unrealistic ideologies.

Don't compare the old to the new. For those of us who are afforded the privilege of remarriage, the worst thing we can do is go into our new relationship comparing our new spouse to a previous partner. Comparisons are natural inclinations, but it must be consciously avoided. Undoubtedly, there may have been things our ex-spouse did wonderfully. Perhaps they knew just how to prepare a favorite meal, connect well with in-laws, or perform well intimately. No matter how great those benefits were, the marriage has now ended, and it ended for a reason. It's time to let go – even if what we are releasing was one of our favorite things. Many of us know the all too painful and familiar feeling of outgrowing our favorite clothes. Letting go of the previous relationship is far worse than that once favorite go-to clothing piece. Our need to moving on from the past is not because we no longer like that item, but because we've literally grown passed that stage. In fact, to continue wearing clothing that doesn't fit is sure to make anyone uncomfortable. It's a horrible feeling when the thing we used to love now makes us uncomfortable, embarrassed and humiliated. Even if we are in our own personal denial, the world can see when we're wearing something that no longer properly fits. We may be the last to see it or admit it, but the world will opinionatedly observe whatever we are not willing to deal with. According to the-late Johnny Cochran, "If it doesn't fit, you must acquit." Ultimately we're trying to place emphasis on giving our new spouse a chance to experience new favorite things with us. We will not have had all of the memories and experiences with our new love, as we had with our ex, so it will take intention. Making new discoveries, with and about our new spouses, will be part of the journey. Our marital satisfaction only climaxes to higher levels we use the past as a stepping stone rather than a stumbling block.

CHAMPIONS IN MARRIAGE
Questions & Discussion
Chapter 4: Remarriage

1. In what ways do you compare your current love to your ex?

2. What steps can you take to give this relationship a clean slate?

3. How do you want this relationship to be different from your past?

_____

_____

_____

_____

_____

_____

_____

Chapter 5
SEX and INTIMACY

Sex is one of God's greatest ideas for marriage. From the beginning of time, God established husband and wife for the purpose of procreation, bonding and mutual fulfillment. A great summary of the purposes and benefits of sex within the confines of marriage is found in: *familytoday.com.* The article is entitled "Why God Created Sex," by author Bob Lepine. He says there are five important reasons why sex is important in marriage:

> 1. *"Sex is meant to strengthen the marriage bond. In marriage we enter into a covenant relationship with one another. This covenant mirrors God's covenant."* He continues explaining *"God wants the husband and wife to be one. The recurring, ongoing participation in sex is the instrument that God uses so that we can experience a closer, richer, deeper relationship with one another."*

Sex is designed to offer us the highest level of fulfillment – mind, body and soul. Even given the physical composition of man and woman, our bodies are meant to connect like a plug to a socket. The male anatomy is created to give and the female anatomy is created to receive and ultimately conceive. Furthermore, during this process of connecting, there is a literal transfer of DNA. Scientists agree, this transfer of DNA stays with us, not just for conception, but many times it enters the bloodstream, organs and brain of the female. The DNA is said to stay with her for a lifetime and beyond (see *familytoday.com*).

The transfer of DNA lasts for a lifetime. There are many studies that suggest that DNA stored by a woman can influence the genetic makeup of unborn children for years to come. In other words, some studies suggest that while a woman can have a baby with her current spouse, the child may carry genes and characteristics of an ex. Sex is so much more than a one-time physical connection. It is designed to be a life-long infusion of the soul of one person with another. Thus, sex is best explored and experienced within the confines of marriage.

2. *"God wants to teach us more about the relationship between the Father, the Son, and the Spirit in the Trinity. There is oneness within the Trinity—there are three persons, but they are one. In marriage, there are two persons, but they become one. In marriage we learn something about the intimacy that God enjoys within the context of the Trinity—the intimacy that the Father has with the Son, and the Son with the Spirit, and the Spirit with the Father and the Son."*

Sex is a model for how two can become one. This one act called sex is the closest comparison we could ever have to understanding the function and purpose of the trinity. Many of us believe in the concept of God possessing three separate entities, Father, Son and Holy Spirit. Together, they function as one. Likewise, during sexual intercourse, a husband and wife connect in much the same way. Couples are two separate individuals that merge as one in mind, body and spirit. Mark 10:8-9 says, *"and the two shall become one flesh'; so then they are no longer two, but one flesh. Therefore, what God has joined together, let not man separate."*

> 3. *"God also wants to give us a picture of Christ's relationship with the Church (Ephesians 5:22-33). In some mysterious way, the husband and wife relationship—and our sexuality—is tied to that picture."*

Our sex life should be mutual, reciprocal and respectful. Consider Ephesians 5:22-33 in the Message Version Bible, *"Wives, understand and support your husbands in ways that show your support for Christ. The husband provides leadership to his wife the way Christ does to his church, not by domineering but by* *cherishing. So just as the church submits to Christ as he exercises such leadership, wives should likewise submit to their husbands."*

From this passage we see that as husband and wife should be mutually consenting. Each plays a part in supporting the other. In addition, marriage and sex should be reciprocal. One shouldn't be more concerned or participatory than the other. Finally, our marriage and sex life as modeled by the illustration of Christ and His church – should be respectful. God doesn't force himself on us, and we shouldn't force our way with each other. Instead, we should submit ourselves one to another, lovingly yielding our bodies for the pleasure of our spouse. This will not only require the ultimate level of vulnerability, but also of mutual respect. If we find ourselves in relationships that are not mutual, reciprocal and respectful, we must seek God and counseling as to how to navigate this dynamic. These circumstances can be complicated and equally as detrimental as abuse and adultery. We empathize with such scenarios. While no one should feel forced to live life in this situation, it does not validate extramarital affairs or divorce.

4. "A sexual relationship in marriage teaches us something about the nature of real love—God's love. Over a lifetime in marriage, we learn that in order for our sexuality to be expressed in the way that God intends it, the sexuality needs to be unselfish. Both husband and wife must be committed to pleasing each other and meeting each other's needs.

Sex, at its best is unselfish. I Corinthians 7:4 says *"The wife does not have authority over her own body but yields it to her husband. In the same way, the husband does not have authority over his own body but yields it to his wife."* This passage is not abrasive, cruel, or justification of rape or the overpowering of one's will over the other. In fact, the opposite is true. This passage illustrates the beauty and grace in yielding ourselves to one another. The unselfish and intimate surrendering of our bodies to our spouse is one of the most expressive ways that we can demonstrate trust and love. When it is reciprocated, we are in full demonstration of Christ's love. He so loved us that he gave. In return, because we love Him, we willingly and lovingly surrender our lives to him and each other. It's not an obligation, it's the ultimate loving choice.

5. It is best for the offspring of our sexual union to grow up in a home governed by a covenant relationship between a husband and a wife who love one another and are committed to each other. If a child is growing up in a setting where there is one parent or where two parents are not bound together in covenant love with one another, that child is missing something.

The enemy desires to pervert human sexuality and destroy future generations. When sex results in procreation, there is an awesome opportunity present to model Christ, His love for us and his design for the family. We are living in a time where single-parent families are not just the norm, in many case they are the preferences. More men and women are frequently opting to parent without having a mate in mind. In our society this is a conscious decision. In fact, many prefer not to co-parent or co-exist. Raising children, without modeling God's desire for family, is blindsiding them. There are invaluable lessons that only marriage can provide. Family is meant to reflect the independent and interdependent relationship of one husband, one wife and their children. Sex is best engaged as an act between two people, not multiple partners, toys and other creative explorations. Sex is meant to illustrate the unselfish giving aspect of submission of yourself to another. It is having those feelings and acts reciprocated and respected. These are principles that have to be modeled to future generations. Otherwise, we run the risk of losing the benefits of God's design for marriage and family.

While we've shared 5 thoughts on sex and intimacy, as presented by Author Bob Alpine, we'd also like to leave you with 3 quick thoughts of our own.

1. **Intimacy is like a fine wine. It should get better with age.** Think about it, there should be a ripening process. The more we get to know our spouse and explore their bodies, desires and preferences, we should become such connoisseurs of our mates that nobody knows them better than us and Christ. If our spouse's mother, sibling(s), or best of friends claim to know our spouse better than we do, that can lead to problems. Just like when we buy a new electronic device, the learning or beginner stages are trial and error. A lot of pushing buttons, hoping something will happen, but not sure what triggers what. However, after we've been married a while, if the communication is effective and the sex acts are unselfish and reciprocal, we should ultimately become masters at what makes our spouse respond. We should hold a private remote control that causes a response no one else could ever imagine exists. The exploration and maturation of our sex lives should be one of the sweetest and most rewarding benefits of our marriage relationship.

2. **Let's find our spouse's "formula" and stick to it.** Throughout school we experience hundreds of students of every age and stage. Those students are given lockers to store belongings. The locker combination for every individual is unique and private. The process keeps everyone's belongings safe and secure. Likewise, our sex life and intimacy with our spouses should be of such privacy and individuality. No one else should ever be able to duplicate the combination or crack the code. The mastery of our spouse's bodies and preferences should be to such a degree that we know a formula and combination that can only be accessed by us. Our continual prayer is that infidelity won't be a temptation or consideration in our marriages. We should possess a formula within our homes and bedrooms that simply cannot be duplicated.

3. **Be flexible. Be creative. Be consistent.** When it comes to sex and intimacy in our marriages we have to face the facts early. We will encounter many seasons and changes, physically, emotionally and ultimately sexually. The key to longevity, is to adapt the mindset, from the start, of flexibility, creativity and consistency. Flexibility means the mental adaptability and perception to know when your routine must be altered. Sometimes, due to physical reasons

(menstruations, illness, pregnancy, female or male complications) life changes. As a result, your sex life will change in various seasons. Whether temporary or permanent, life is bound to interrupt the regularly scheduled program of our sex life. This doesn't mean there has to necessarily be a stop in action, just be flexible. Don't be afraid to change things up. Whenever and however necessary be flexible.

Changes in life, and thus our sex life, may also require creativity. Our spouse may find themselves having to travel for work and adjusting to shift changes. Many times in life, we find ourselves like ships passing in the night. Ultimately, no matter what the cause of the circumstance, we have to find a way for our ships to dock. This requires creativity. Rather than outlining a myriad of potential scenarios, we will allow you to use your creativity. Explore ways that you can ensure there is no breach in action, even amidst changes of schedule and circumstance. Allow your ship to dock.

Finally, in order to preserve and maintain our ideal sex and intimacy life, we must be consistent. It's funny how couples start off blowing each other's mind. But that same couple, over time, barely blow out the candle – let alone light it. Inevitably, as life and years move forward, things tend to settle into a norm. We often find ourselves in a place that may not be as passionate, vibrant or frequent as it was during the early years of the marriage. Still, we have both the challenge and responsibility to find a formula and routine that completely fulfills both spouses long-term. Once we find that rhythm, come hell or high water, we must be intentional about consistency. When we follow this formula we can expect consistent results.

CHAMPIONS IN MARRIAGE
Questions & Discussion
Chapter 5: Sex & Intimacy

1. How would you rate your current sex life with your spouse on a scale from 1-10?

2. What would need to happen to move your score closer to a 10?

3. What can be done to improve your level of true intimacy?

_____

_____

_____

_____

_____

_____

_____

_____

Chapter 6
BUILDING CORE COMMONALITIES

All we need Is love – right? In 1967, the iconic band The Beatles released a song called "All You Need Is Love," written by John Lennon and Paul McCarthy. At a time of war and immense hatred, this legendary band premiered this song to over 400 million people in 25 different countries. It was the first ever live, international, satellite television production, which was broadcast on June 25, 1967. The song was written during the height of the Vietnam War, as an antidote to remind an angry culture to remember love and peace. The sentiment of the song was ideological. The lyrics were simple, "All you need is love. Love is all you need." The concept of love is so beautiful, universal and widely understood that in an ideal world, the Beatles were right. Love should be all we need. The presence of Love should just be enough to heal all, solve all the world's problems, and make everything work. Love should be all we need. Unfortunately, the painful truth is, in life and in marriage, Love is not all we need. In fact, nearly 10 years later, another song emerged that challenged whether love had any relevance to our relationships at all.

What's Love Got to do with It? Tina Turner famously coined the phrase "What's Love Got to do with it"? First released as a song in 1984, then as a blockbuster movie in 1993, "What's Love Got to Do with It" became the self-proclaimed anthem of Tina

Turner and the sentiment of many who have fallen and failed in love. The lyrics say:

What's love got to do, got to do with it
What's love but a second hand emotion
What's love got to do, got to do with it
Who needs a heart when a heart can be broken?

This song highlights the realities that sometimes, no matter how much you love a person, love alone does not prevent a heart from being broken. Love, alone, does not keep a relationship or marriage intact. There are a whole lot more ingredients that go into making a successful relationship survive. One of those staple commodities is building core commonalities.

It's totally possible to be together, but grow apart. Many of us have witnessed or experienced the tragedy of growing apart. Long term relationships sometimes spiral from close knit connections to having nothing in common. Every relationship needs maintenance and new experiences to keep it thriving and relevant. There are friends of ours that bring smiles to our faces at the mention of their name. They remind us of good times and old memories. Often times, however, if new experiences aren't created, twenty-years later all we'll be able to talk about are decades of old memories. Fond memories of old friends aren't enough to keep us connected – chances are, without interacting distant friends may fade away. With every new year people gradually change. The love may not diminish, but the strength of the bond may be tested. In this way, marriage exceeds the standard friendship. It is absolutely possible to live with, sleep beside and love someone for years and not get an update on who they are becoming. When communication stops growth stops. Life changes. People change. Likewise, as spouses, we have to be intentionally and regularly connect and communicate about things that matter to one another.

Believe as one and go to church together. The very foundation of building core commonalities is sharing the same faith. There are bound to be many disagreements and varying viewpoints between spouses concerning our beliefs. One of the most potentially detrimental and divisive roadblocks in a marriage is not sharing the same beliefs and core practices. A recent article featured in *Focusonthefamily.com* evaluated a compilation of studies from leading sociologists and marriage and family experts. The studies evaluated Christian marriage and divorce rates and current trends. According to this particular article, "The divorce rate among Christians is significantly lower than the general population." It further went on to explain that "Couples who regularly practice any combination of serious religious behaviors and attitudes – attend church nearly every week, read their Bibles and spiritual materials regularly; pray privately and together; generally, take their faith seriously, living not as perfect disciples, but serious disciples – enjoy significantly lower divorce rates than mere church members, the general public and unbelievers."

As part of this study, Professor Bradley Wright, a sociologist at the University of Connecticut, explains from his analysis of people who identify as Christians but rarely attend church, that 60 percent of these couples have been divorced. Of those who attend church regularly, only 38 percent have been divorced. Other data from additional sociologists of family and religion suggest a significant marital stability divide between those who take their faith seriously and those who do not.

Also as part of this study, Professor Scott Stanley from the University of Denver, working with an absolute all-star team of leading sociologists on the Oklahoma Marriage Study concluded that couples with a vibrant religious faith had more and higher levels of the qualities couples need to avoid divorce.

"Whether young or old, male or female, low-income or not, those who said that they were more religious reported higher average levels of commitment to their partners, higher levels of marital satisfaction, less thinking and talking about divorce and lower levels of negative interaction. These patterns held true when controlling for such important variables as income, education, and age at first marriage."

- Professor Scott Stanley

Look for all the ways we are similar and draw upon them. No two people in God's creation are identical, even identical twins have distinguishing fingerprints and personality traits. Likewise, even the strongest most compatible couple will have differences in opinions and approaches. Our challenge is not to focus on the differences, but find the commonalities.

Perhaps its a love of music, television or gourmet cooking. Whatever those similarities are, be it sports, long walks, or dancing, we should take note and incorporate them into our everyday life. Why is this so important? Because inevitably the season will come that will make you question, "Why did I get marry?" "My spouse just doesn't get me." Having a well of commonalities to draw from helps during difficult times. It will work wonders in reconnecting and reminding us of how we fell in love and the many reasons we enjoy being married – yes, even healthy marriages need reminders.

Focus on the majors, not the minors. Perhaps you've heard the saying, "It's the little foxes that spoil the vine?" Well, it's true. Many times, our marriages hit our breaking point. It usually happens over minor details, not major mistakes. Major blow ups are often a result of the accumulation of a million little unresolved disagreements, differences and annoyances. A hundred little things will one day equal the same potential detriment of one huge indiscretion. That's why we must address small concerns and let them go quickly.

People change, feelings change - stay up to date. Change is natural, normal and necessary – it can also be uncomfortable. As we discussed earlier in this chapter, it is important that we keep up with the ever-growing, ever-evolving thoughts, feelings and preferences of our spouses. Let's not be so quick to say "I know her/him like the back of my hand". Odds are if we don't maintain core commonalities you won't know our spouses like we think we do. Unlike inanimate objects or pieces of furniture, human beings are complex individuals comprised of many varying and evolving thoughts and feelings. Let's examine an illustration of this point. At age 10 what was your hair like? Would you wear that same hairstyle today? Now, picture the clothes you had on. Whatever you were wearing, would you wear that today? Most hilariously, now picture the boy/girl you liked at that age. Do you think that is the person you would choose as your spouse today? In most cases, the answer is an emphatic no! Why? Aren't we the same person now as we were then? Why are our preferences now so drastically different? The answer is simple - we have evolved. Growth and evolvement occurs steadily, slowly and sometimes rapidly everyday of our lives. In many cases, people don't realize when character changes occur without reminiscing. We are always evolving. Without effort, our thoughts, beliefs, preferences and desires are changing everyday based on experiences and exposure. The intoxicating cologne and perfume fragrances from twenty-years-ago are now overpowering, outdated and unappealing. Our preferences change. We absolutely, positively must discuss with our spouse when our preferences change, so that they are growing and evolving with us.

Schedule time for a check-up and check-in. When we have children, The American Academy of Pediatrics recommends that we take our baby in for at least nine checkups during the first three years. When our babies become toddlers, doctors recommend at least 3 more. As we become older, the recommendation is that we have a check-up at least once a year, for as long as we are alive. The check-ups are not only to screen our current health; they are also for preventative care. They identify traces of something growing in our bodies that might adversely affect our health. As a result, we have the potential to reverse it and hopefully keep it from occurring again. Likewise, our relationships require routine maintenance and preventative care. We need to do a periodic check-up to gauge the health of our marriage. Is there a cancer of disagreement growing that we are unaware of? Those seemingly minor uncommunicated concerns and wavering thoughts have the potential to spread like cancer. Perhaps there's an unsettled issue that is festering and harboring in our hearts against our spouses. Whatever it is, however small it may appear, a marital check-up is always in order. Don't be afraid of confrontation – for more tips on how to communicate with your spouse refer to chapter 11, *Personality Differences and Communication Styles.* Have meetings, ask questions and express concerns. If we disconnect by failing to communicate concerning difficult subject matters, we'll render your relationship powerless. Communication is a primary pillar of all relationships.

Similarly, check-ins are also in order. A check-in allows us to get a current status check of our mate's likes and dislikes. Check-ins also enable us to identify changes in our preferences. It is extremely important that when we check-in, we are brutally honest. Most of us want to please our spouses. It's never our desire to fall short or be less than what our partner needs. Let's not wait until a heated argument to surprise or sabotage our spouse with new information about ourselves or how we feel about them. In a marriage, it is always both parties' personal responsibility not only to verbalize our preferences, but to request updates from our spouses. No marriage can end without both individuals owning an aspect of the failure – communication is a two-way-street. Sometimes we have to read the sign language, yield to unexpected changes, anticipate detours and listen for warnings. The details matter when we're spending our lives with someone. From breakfast to the bedroom, no conversation should be off limits. Let's embrace the logic, "If it's important to you, it's important to me" – everything should always remain open for discussion. Let's always make our spouses feel like their opinions, thoughts and concerns are relevant. Otherwise, avoiding uncomfortable dialog can potentially tear at the fabric of our marriages.

CHAMPIONS IN MARRIAGE
Questions & Discussion
Chapter 6: Building Core Commonalities

1. What kinds of interests/activities do you and your spouse enjoy doing together?

2. If those interests/activities were not in place, how different do you think your marriage would be?

3. How can you be more intentional about sharing, interests and activities?

_____

_____

_____

_____

_____

_____

_____

_____

Chapter 7
Blended Family:
Step-Parenting, Raising Somebody Else's Child

Children are a blessing from God. We've heard those words so often that it can almost sound a bit cliché. It's true. When God chooses us to parent children and have influence over how they live, grow and develop, it's a gift. In biblical accounts, the angel Gabriel appeared to Mary, the mother of Jesus, to tell her that she was going to become a mom. Strikingly, the first thing Gabriel said to her was *"Hail, Thou that art highly favored, the Lord is with thee: blessed art thou among women"* (Luke 1:27). It is quite notable that the angel emphasized to Mary that becoming a mother would be a position of favor. He knew she would need those reassurances along the way. As with Mary, the same is true for every person that is positioned to parent a child. It is an honor that is divinely bestowed upon us, and we can rest assured that we will not be in this journey alone – God is with us. This remains especially true for those who are chosen to raise children in blended families. Those of us who make the choice to parent non-biological children are modeling Christ's concept concerning adoption. In this case, we're not referring to the legal term of adoption, rather the relational aspect of what it means to adopt. Defined by Merriam-Webster dictionary, to adopt is *"to take by choice into a relationship"*. In the Old Testament, we learn that the world had become so wicked that it was decided that man would be wiped off the face of the earth. This meant we would be out of fellowship with God. Instead, He loved us so much that He didn't want to exist without us, so he chose to send his only Son, Jesus, to reconcile us to *Himself* through adoption. This spiritual adoption gave us the rights, privileges and joint inheritance of Jesus. Would you offer your only perfect, sinless and blameless child as a sacrifice for issue-ridden, ungrateful and problematic children? That's what kind of love God had for us. Likewise, there a special grace for individuals who emulate *His* selflessness in parenting. When we selflessly choose assume the responsibilities of raising a child, we model Christ's love for the world. We just have to be sober-minded and aware that while we try to exemplify Christ, we are not quite that inherently kind, good or selfless. Unlike God, as parent we make mistakes. It demands a lot of of intention, attention and preparation to parent children we do not birth. We have to prepare our hearts to love the child, and in some cases multiple children. We must also carve out time and allow opportunities for them to prepare their hearts for us.

We should prepare children for a new parent figure. As early as humanly possible, when a new family is going to be formed that will include step, foster, guardianship or adopted children, we should consider involving them in premarital counseling. This kind of family planning will safeguard blended families from becoming blindsided by unexpected disappointments. Pre-marital family counseling will empower everyone to verbalize expectations. In the case of inheriting step-children, many couples make a common mistake. They have lengthy dating periods, commit to a life of love and prepare for marriage prior to involving existing children. While there are no standardized rules on how this should be done, we should give children an opportunity to adjust. Listen to their input. Be considerate enough to recognize that they are a part of the family. In most cases, children view the new spouse as the add on to the family, not themselves. Remember, the children were there first. Instead of making them feel like someone has stolen their parent, we should try using loving-kindness to become another parent-figure to them. The more we make the children feel a part of the process, the more invested they become to the entire family.

Establish ground rules and parent/child role responsibilities. Establishing expectations work wonders when raising children. Whether in a work or family setting, people best excel in environments where there is a clarification of roles and responsibilities. Where expectations are set, they have the opportunity to be met. Everything from household chores to role classifications should be discussed from the inception of a new family, especially when children are involved. Just like adults, children of all ages and stages feel a sense of accomplishment when they know what to do and are able to do it. The less intimidated children are by their new parents and family structure, the more open they become. Hence, they freely navigate until they discover a comfortable disposition in the family. Parent roles are also important to discuss and establish upfront. Will both parents be allowed to discipline the child? Discipline requires discussion, relationship and a detailed understanding of a child's history. Discipline must be handled delicately, otherwise you can ruin a child emotionally, socially and psychologically. When discipline is too much, too little or too careless, blended families can become explosive minefields. Seek professional family counseling prior to marriage. Don't just go with the flow, discuss the kind of expectations that will create a productive current to foster a healthy household.

Build a support system that reinforces agreed structure. Establishing roles and understandings aren't just important internally. It's important that family members, friends and educators understand these roles. Being affirmed in our new role is priceless. When we have supportive people in our lives that are helping by echoing like-minded language to our children, it is invaluable. The African proverb says *"It takes a* *village to raise a child"*. That proverb has proven true time and time again. It's important that the entire village is resonating the same message and embracing basic principles. Agreement is a powerful force. In contrast, teaching children not to use profanity, but surrounding them with loved ones that swear like sailors is counterproductive. It not only sends mixed messages, but it also undermines family values. We cannot control what happens outside our home, but we must be accountable to the influences and standards we allow. We must create a village of like-minded thinkers. Most well-intentioned people in our lives want to help us in the rearing of healthy children, and would take no issue with treating our children the way we do.

We must choose to love non-biological children like they are our own – everyday. Love is ultimately a choice. We can choose to extend and display love or withhold it. In most cases, raising someone else's child, is of no fault of the child. Whether we gain our new children by marriage, death, drugs, abuse or other circumstances, we must remember that the child is walking into a situation innocently. The acceptance and adjustment of having a new parent can be life-altering. It is our adult responsibility to do everything within reason to make children feel safe and accepted. This won't always be easy, but it will be worth it. Always remember they are children, no matter how good or bad their deeds at times – we must choose to love them.

Rebound from rejection. Expect children to test your patience. In our new roles as caregivers, we must avoid wearing our emotions on our sleeves. In a new family dynamic, it's easy to focus on our feelings – and worthless at the same time. We must put ourselves in the position of the child. The acceptance and adjustment to having an unknown parent-figure can be daunting. While we may be jumping through hoops to win their favor, expect some initial rejection – it's natural. Don't take everything personal – the child's feelings aren't necessarily all about you.

An article entitled "Living with Step-parents," on *kidshealth.org* explored the many feelings children have when trying to adjust to a new parent. The article explains how children may not be able to stop wishing that things were the way they were before. Children usually agree that their feelings are a spiral of mixed emotions. The displacement and lack of loyalty or clarity of the role of their biological parent is often difficult to process. In addition, sharing televisions, bathrooms and meals can create an ill sense of belonging for children trying to find their footing. Oftentimes, children need adults to help them figure out exactly where their feelings are spiraling from. We must empower our children and make them feel comfortable enough to speak up in a judgment-free atmosphere. It's not easy sharing a parent and a home with a step-parent or family member. It can be even more difficult if the step-parent has children. In a healthy functional family environment, children must feel equally validated, supported and loved.

Don't resent or lash out at children because of their parent. Without even realizing it, there may be times we feel frustrated, even resentful of carrying someone else's load. Shouldering unforeseen responsibilities can create vexations. These nuisances can cause new parents to beat themselves up. This reality is common, but unacceptable – always remember, our effort is honorable and God is with us. We must resist tendencies to voice our opinions about the child's biological parents. Know that whatever we feel about their non-present parent has nothing to do with our relationship with the child. Let's be quick to listen, slow to speak and find healthy mechanisms to cope with our frustrations.

CHAMPIONS IN MARRIAGE
Questions & Discussion
Chapter 7: Blended Families

1. If placed in a position where you had to step in and assist in raising someone else's child, how well do you think you could adjust to that responsibility?

2. In filling this role, what would be your major concerns and/or deal-breakers?

3. What kind of support would you need to be successful in this endeavor?

_____

_____

_____

_____

_____

_____

_____

_____

Chapter 8
In Sickness and in Health

Honor **your vows, no matter what**. During traditional wedding ceremonies, every couple expresses vows. In the presence of our family and friends, ministers officiate as grooms and brides recite vows similar to this:

> *"I, _____, take you, _____, to be my wife/husband, to have and to hold from this day forward, for better, for worse, for richer, for poorer, in sickness and in health, to love and to cherish, until we are parted by death. This is my solemn vow."*

Happily-ever-after isn't a reality of most. While we are standing there gazing into each other's eyes, most of us are not really taking in and conceptualizing the full magnitude of these words. We are imagining our happily-ever-after. We are captured in the feelings of that day. We are looking forward to the *first* kiss, the jumping of the broom, the reception, *first* dance, pictures, frisky limo ride to the airport, getting to our hotel and the romances of the night. The thought of difficult days fade into a distant reality, for newlyweds. The reality is, we enter into this agreement with optimistic expectations. Then life happens. Many of us will find ourselves facing the better *and* worse, the richer *and* poorer, the health *and* sickness without counting the cost. Some couples even encounter the death-do-us-part long before anticipated.

In 2015, *The Journal of Health and Social Behavior* gathered data on 2,701 married couples in an article entitled "In Sickness and Health". The study was conducted by Amelia Karraker, Iowa State assistant professor of human development, and Kenzie Latham, Indiana/Purdue University Department of Sociology. The analysis followed married couples over a 20-year timespan. During this period, a large percentage of the couples encountered everything from cancer, heart disease, lung disease and stroke. The findings revealed that 32-percent of those marriages ended in divorce and 24-percent ended due to the death of a spouse. The study also revealed that husbands falling ill had no effect on divorce rates, but sick wives resulted in 6-percent more divorces. Divorce was more common amongst younger couples and widowhood was more common among older couples.

Based on this 20-year study, we understand that difficult times are not only likely, they may be inevitable. We must prepare for unexpected and unwanted realities before saying "I do".

True love and commitment can overpower any sickness and disease. It is quite possible that at some point in our marriage, due to no fault of our own, our bodies may fail us. Whether it is an unforeseen illness or tragic accident, many couples will face the grueling aspects of their vows – sometimes sickness and death. However, illness and disease are no match for two committed people who sincerely love one another. We've listed a couple of amazing stories of couples whose love outlasted even death itself. We thought you might enjoy them as much as we did.

Tom and Naomi Shirley

From: Southwest Ranches, Florida

Married for: 45 years

How they met: When Tom was working as a game warden in the Florida Everglades, he stopped at a drug store where Shirley worked. The couple quickly discovered a shared love for the outdoors. The adventure seekers were inseparable during their marriage as they raised four children. They explored the Florida and other distant locations together. Both Tom and Shirley had a strong connection to the Everglades where they loved air boating and camping. They were dedicated to preserving it for future generations.

Their enduring love story: In 2018, Tom was hospitalized for heart trouble. As Shirley was being driven from her home to visit him, she also suffered a heart attack and passed away. Unknown to Shirley, Tom had passed away just 15 minutes earlier in the hospital. The couple never learned of the other's passing and were both spared the pain of losing their spouse. The legacy they left behind includes four children and eight grandchildren.

Gordon and Norma Yeager
From: State Center, Iowa
Married for: 72 Years
How they met: Gordon and Norma were lifelong companions who rarely left each other's side. In 1939, the couple got married within 12 hours of their engagement on the day of Norma's high school graduation. For more than seven decades, Gordon and Norma traveled, worked and raised their two children together. They even participated in the same clubs and ran family businesses remaining close to one another at all times.

Their enduring love story: Norma and Gordon spent their lives side-by-side and that is the same way they left this world. The couple was driving into town when a car accident sent them both to the hospital with injuries. Both Norma and Gordon were highly concerned about one another, asking their children how the other was doing until it became clear to the hospital they should be moved into the same room. According to witnesses which included family and hospital staff, when Gordon's breathing stopped, his heart still continued beating on the monitors. It wasn't until Norma passed an hour later that it finally stopped, leading their loved ones to believe that Gordon waited so they could enter the afterlife together.

Fight for your new normal. Don't compare your marriage to everyone else's. Sometimes you have to dig deep to discover a new normal in order to make your marriage work. A new normal has the potential to breath new life into marriages. Life after illness may not be as glamorous, sexy or ideal as we imagined. It is possible to find a new normal that works for both parties.

For example, for various reasons, husbands may find their ability to achieve a sustained erection challenging because erectile dysfunction. Likewise, wives, may endure procedures and treatments that may result in vaginal dryness or loss of desire. Find a work-around. Don't give up. There may even be a renewed sense of adventure in exploring new methods of sexual intimacy and connection. The point is, we must make up in our minds, from the time we first say our vows that nothing will part us but death itself. For each couple, finding a new normal will look different, but with true love and commitment all things are possible.

Keep an attitude of gratitude. No matter how bad it gets, it could be worse – and it can get better. We don't know the gravity of your situation, but what we do know is, no matter how bad your situation is, there is a place of peace and contentment that you can find, especially in Christ. We've all been in some difficult places. Let's ponder the following verses from the Bible:

"Not that I speak from [any personal] need, for I have learned to be content [and self-sufficient through Christ, satisfied to the point where I am not disturbed or uneasy] regardless of my circumstances. 12 I know how to get along and live humbly [in difficult times], and I also know how to enjoy abundance and live in prosperity. In any and every circumstance I have learned the secret [of facing life], whether well-fed or going hungry, whether having an abundance or being in need. 13 I can do all things [which He has called me to do] through Him who strengthens and empowers me [to fulfill His purpose—I am self-sufficient in Christ's sufficiency; I am ready for anything and equal to anything through Him who infuses me with inner strength and confident peace]" Philippians 4:11-13 Amplified Bible (AMP).

CHAMPIONS IN MARRIAGE
Questions & Discussion
Chapter 8: In Sickness & In Health

1. Imagine an unforeseen accident that has detrimental effects on your spouse. To what extent could you see yourself being a primary caregiver?

2. What support would you need to do it long-term?

3. Discuss ways you could remain intimate with your spouse, if they had physical limitations to your current sex life?

_____

_____

_____

_____

_____

_____

_____

_____

CHAPTER 9
The Case for Counseling

Counseling Corrects Conflict. No matter how madly in love a husband and wife may be, it is inevitable that human beings will have different opinions. Differences of opinion often lead to conflict – but conflict is not necessarily negative. Conflict can be useful and healthy in a marriage relationship because it teaches us the art of validating and valuing one another's perspectives. We are made to walk as one, not to literally morph into one. The perfect harmony is created when two separate individuals function as a whole by aligning themselves as one. Marriage creates a melody that could not be achieved independently. Coming to a place of achieving harmony without conformity sometimes require counseling. In this effort, a counselor is able to help each party embrace perspectives while listening and hearing one another's thoughts and feelings. This may seem easy for us to accomplish alone, but not necessarily. Escalating tones and tempers and heated emotions often spiral into situations that demand a mediator.

Counseling or Crutches. Without the benefit of counseling, we can easily develop crutches to cope with critical circumstances. Some of us turn to food, alcohol or drugs. Others turn to hyperactivities like working extended hours or becoming a gym rat. Some turn to religion or other seemingly positive outlets. When used in excess or as a means of avoidance for life's issues, these endeavors become crutches. Counseling is a significant source to reduce the need for crutches. Counseling forces us to identify, address and disarm our demons. Counseling is helpful in eliminating our crutches in any relationship, but especially in marriage. In marriage, a husband and wife should be able to go to each other as a primary confidante, secret keeper and first line of defense. However, we must remove the crutches in the way, i.e. best friends, parents, co-workers or old high school buddies as preferred sources. Otherwise, we will find ourselves strengthening outside relationships while weakening our marriages. Counseling helps couples deal with small subjects before they become bigger, less manageable issues.

Counseling Cures Cancers. In essence, cancer is a disease caused by an uncontrolled division of abnormal cells in a part of the body. In our relationships and marriages, cancer is caused when there is uncontrolled division. In marriage, we may encounter abnormalities, but they do not have to destroy the relationship. It's when the relationship becomes uncontrollably divided that there needs to be urgent professional intervention. Once a cancer, of any type, has set in and spread, it is no longer manageable by self-care. There needs to be corrective therapy administered to begin the process of eliminating the cancer. Counseling is a therapy that helps couples identify what is unhealthy and what is dividing the relationship. Counseling contains the issue, stops it from spreading and counteracts the death of a marriage. Through marriage counseling, we are better able to correctly shift our focus away from our partners and focus on becoming a better individual.

Counseling Clarifies Character. When life goes wrong, it's human nature to point the blame. It's like there's a part of us that just has to make the situation somebody's fault. Have you ever watched a movie or heard a story of someone dying unexpectedly? If the deceased is older and wealthy, and the surviving spouse is young, foul play is immediately suspected. We need someone to blame. "It's her fault." "It's his fault." Sometimes it's nobody's fault. There is just a problem or issue that needs to be fixed. When trying to make two wonderfully designed components function as one, complications are likely. However, engineering the end result can prove priceless – power couples often require the most most challenges fixes. You might not know how to fix it on your own – and that's ok. God places people in our lives to help us in ways that we can't figure on our own. Utilizing our God-given resources provides a peace and calm amid life's storms.

Counseling Calms Couples. Knowing that there is a fix to a problem can immediately calm tension and anxiety. Even before the problem itself is actually solved, hope offers a sense of healing. For example, if you discover a water leak in your home, you may initially panic or experience feelings of disgust. The moment the plumber assures that they are in route with a resolve, a calmness occurs. Not that the problem is immediately fixed, but there is a calm in knowing help is on the way. That's what counseling does for couples, it reassures us that the problem won't take us under – help is on the way. There is a light at the end of the tunnel. Think about how many marriages fail due to irreconcilable differences. In other words, the divorce spiraled from an inability to find a solution or happy medium to marital issues. Counseling can often be a divine answer to that. It's calming and reassuring for couples to know that nothing we face is insurmountable, unfixable or unsolvable. There is a remedy or formula for nearly everything we face. We often just need help identifying and applying it to our marriages. Marriages are salvageable with the right support. There's nothing wrong with seeking help and advice. The wisest people in the world have learned this truth, and are the better for it.

CHAMPIONS IN MARRIAGE
Questions & Discussion
Chapter 9: The Case for Counseling

1. Have you ever participated in couple's/marital counseling?

2. What, if any, are your concerns or apprehensions about counseling?

3. What might be the potential benefits of counseling to your relationship?

_____

_____

_____

_____

_____

_____

_____

_____

_____

CHAPTER 10
Building Your Inner Circle:
Friendships, Mentors & Associates

It is not good for man to be alone. From the beginning of time, there has always been a need for man to have companionship and camaraderie. From the very first book of the Bible, we see God's plan for marriage and companionship. Genesis 2:18 says, *"And the Lord said, it is not good that man should be alone."* Heaven and earth were created. The sun, moon and stars were made. The oceans, mountains and every majestic creature on the planet took its place in the ecosystem. God looked at them and said *"It is good".* Then he formed man, because He wanted a creation that was in His image and likeness, to have dominion, and to be fruitful and blessed. But man was the one creation that *He* looked upon and immediately thought to add to it. *He* said, *"It is not good for man to be alone".* God acknowledged that as wonderful a creation that man is, he needed some help. He would be even more effective, happy and productive if man had a partner. In this life, no matter how great we are, we can always be better with the right support system.

Find people you trust to build your team. Qualify them. Arguably, the 1996 Chicago Bulls team is said to be one of the greatest teams in the 20th century, and possibly of all time. With a season win record of 72-10, finishing 1st in the NBA Central Division, the Chicago Bulls were world-renowned. Not just because of their star athlete, but because of their stellar supportive team. Sure, in 1996 Michael Jordan single-handedly scored 2,491 points, averaging 30.4 points a game, but he was gallantly assisted by a starting line-up that included the likes of all-stars like Scottie Pippen, with 1,496 pts, and Tony Kukoc, with 1,065 pts, not to mention Dennis Rodman, Steve Kerr and the list goes on. Michael Jordan is considered by many to be the greatest basketball player of all-time. However, he didn't win 6 championships alone. He needed a team. A good team. A vetted team. A dependable and consistent team. As married couples, our team is as great of a predictor of our success as we are. In life and in marriage, we need a good, vetted, dependable and consistent team to keep us accountable and push us to our best capabilities.

Don't find people that just agree with you, find those that will challenge you. Good friends will not just be our amen corner, they will be our mirrors. They will show us who and where we are, and when we're getting it wrong. This is especially important when we are married because the day will come when we will rely on the input and advice of a friend as to what to do in our relationship. The wrong advice or adviser can mean the difference between success or failure in our marriage.

"Blessed is the man that walketh not in the counsel of the unGodly, nor standeth in the way of sinners, nor sitteth in the seat of the scornful. 2 But his delight is in the law of the Lord; and in his law doth he meditates day and night. 3 And he shall be like a tree planted by the rivers of water, that bringeth forth his fruit in his season; his leaf also shall not wither; and whatsoever he doeth shall prosper. 4 The unGodly are not so: but are like the chaff which the wind driveth away. This set of verses warn of us of the pitfalls and benefit of who we counsel with. We will either flourish like the tree, planted by water or we will wither like the dry and barren chaff. Counsel is crucial, especially when it's kept confidential" (Psalms 1:1-4).

Confidentiality is a necessity. What's the benefit of confiding in a person who can't hold water? Our marriage is one of the most sacred unions we'll ever experience. We must guard it as the fragile and priceless commodity that it is. Thus, in times of hardship and peril, when consulting for advice we need the best, most reliable source. Convenience does not meet the criteria for accommodating the needs of marriages. Let's say, you purchase a 2019 Porsche 911. If in a few months this car begins to experience difficulty, you are not going to take this $100,000 vehicle to your neighborhood fix-it shop. You would demand an authorized specialty dealership for Porsche. With a car that valuable, you want to know that you have placed it in trusted hands. There are certain assurances when taking your car to the right place. Our marriage, our secrets, our embarrassing spats and our vulnerabilities can't be out in the hands of just anyone. We have to have confidence in our friends and confidants, or there's really no value in having them in our circle. The qualification for someone being on our team to support our marriage should be extremely high.

Loyalty: Evaluate them before you trust them. In addition to truthfulness and secrecy, our inner circle must be proven loyalists. Loyalty is the quality of staying firm in your obligation to someone or something, even in the face of adverse circumstances. There is a quote that says, "Blood makes you related, loyalty makes you family". Many times, we find out who our truest supporters are during difficult times. It's easy to be present during the good times, but when our back is against a wall, true friends withstand seasons of adversity. That kind of loyalty should be proven prior to allowing individuals into your inner circle. Proverbs 17:17 (NIV) says, *"A friend loves at all times, and a brother is born for a time of adversity."* Who are your influences? Let's make sure they are not only loyal, but that they also have something to offer. Let's find people that allow us to speak life rather than just speak out. Do they demonstrate love toward your family, or only you? Are they keeping your secrets from your spouse, or helping you and your spouse process the most difficult secrets of your marriage? Don't fool yourself. A loyal friend aims to support your marriage. If you find yourself building a secret relationship with them based on dialog about your spouse, they are not an appropriate team player. Re-evaluate your inner circle.

Mentors: Find someone who is where you're trying to go, not just people you like. By definition, a mentor is a person who guides and advices based on a proven area of mastery and expertise. Having a marriage mentor is as practical as a singer having a vocal coach. Psalm 37:37 says, *"Mark the perfect man and behold the upright: for the end of that man is peace."* In other words, while we know there is no literally perfect person walking amongst us, the essence of this verse encourages us to take note of people who are walking excellently and uprightly. Their story will end the right way. We must identify people who have walked the steps we are trying to achieve, and did it well. As a newlywed, it wouldn't be wise to consider a couple who's only been married a few months as a marriage mentor. They may find themselves in our circle of partners, mutual friends and companions, but not mentors. We shouldn't have to warn you of this, but your marriage mentor certainly should not be single. Marriage mentors should be prayerfully and carefully identified by both spouses, as spiritual accountability partners who help us to grow and mature in areas of our weaknesses. They provide a reassuring and safe outlet for guidance and strength. We can't get through our marriages successfully, alone. We will need a strong, vetted team. Let's be careful to pray and open ourselves to the possibility of a team that God divinely assigns. Allow those particular people into your life.

CHAMPIONS IN MARRIAGE
Questions & Discussion
Chapter 10: Building Your Inner Circle

1. Who are your closest friends?

2. Are your closest friends also friends of your spouse? Why/Why not?

3. Discuss the potential benefits of your closest friends being close with your spouse. Now, discuss the potential pitfalls of then not being close.

_____

_____

_____

_____

_____

_____

_____

_____

CHAPTER 11
Personality Differences and Communication Styles

Women are from Mars, men are from Venus. In 1992, now famous author, John Gray, published the book "Men Are from Mars, Women Are from Venus" and the world went nuts over it. It is the book that captured and validated every couple's thoughts on the vast differences between men and women. The wildly popular book quickly sold more than 15 million copies and was ranked the highest work of non-fiction of the 1990's. It remained on the bestseller list for 121 weeks. This explored the idea that common relationship problems between men and women are a result of fundamental psychological differences between the sexes. For example, one of the major themes Gray addresses in the book is how each gender reacts differently to stress. Gray says, "when men reach the peak of their stress level, they withdraw or retreat into their cave." He says "time-out" lets them distance themselves from the problem and relax. This allows them to re-examine the problem later from a fresh perspective. He continues by explaining the difficult phenomenon for women to understand because they tend to do just the opposite. Gray highlighted, "When women become stressed, their natural reaction is to talk with someone close about it, even if talking doesn't provide a solution to the problem at hand." This, in turn, causes the cantankerous dynamic where the man retreats as the woman tries to get closer, ultimately resulting in a major source of conflict between them.

Opposites that first attract, can also attack. It is common for two people who are opposites to find a connection and attraction. Initially, there are plenty of upsides to having someone be the ying to our yang. It is adventurous and alluring to connect with someone we have such little in common with. The enigmatic surprises are intriguing. These mysterious differences can make us feel alive and passionate about exploring unknown possibilities. It adds a sense of spice to a new love. The problem is, over time, the couple settles into their lives and traditional roles. As a result, impressing one another stops and chaos starts. Don't fret. Such discoveries do not have to be deal breakers. The more we learn about each other, the more we give space for true and lasting commitment and appreciation. Let's be intentional about discovering and celebrating our differences, rather than attacking each other for them. A good first step in this journey of discovery is evaluating our basic personalities. While there is no cookie-cutter umbrella that perfectly categorizes everyone, there are some pretty commonly accepted measurements that will give us a great place to start. One of the more popular used personality assessment tests is the Myers-Briggs Type Indicator Test

(MBIT). Developed by Katharine Cook and her daughter Isabel Briggs-Myers in the early 1940's. The Myers-Briggs Type Indicator Test is based on the *conceptual theory* proposed by Carl Jung who had speculated that humans experience the world using four principle psychological functions – sensation, intuition, feeling and thinking. This theory says that one of these four functions is dominant for a person most of the time. It is said that one day, after meeting her future son-in-law for the first time, she observed marked differences between his personality and that of other family members. This caused Briggs to begin reading biographies. Ultimately, she developed a theory and typology wherein she proposed that humans exhibit four primary temperaments: meditative (or thoughtful), spontaneous, executive, and social. It is said that our stance on each of these four principles determine our overall personality, and there are 16 possible combinations of personality types. Here is a brief explanation of the four dichotomies that make up these possibilities:

- **Introversion and extroversion**: refers to whether you see the world through more of an internal (introversion) or external (extroversion) lens.

- **Sensing and intuition**: tells us if a person gathers information more from the external senses (sensing) or from inner sources like knowledge and imagination (intuition)

- **Thinking and feeling**: this relates to whether you make decisions based on objective (thinking) or subjective (feeling) information

- **Judging and perceiving**: this tells us whether you look at the world through a neat lens of organization and planning (judging) or prefer to keep your worldview more open and flexible (perceiving)

Myers-Briggs Type Indicator Test, offers great discussion and discovery. Again, this test isn't meant to be a one-size-fit-all summary of all people. Having a better understanding of why people are the way they are, helps to better understand and live peaceably with ourselves and the ones we love. Once we have grasped a basic understanding of our personality, the next step is learning how to most effectively communicate.

It's not *what* we say, it's *how* we say it. Many times the key to better understanding and co-existence with our spouse lies in our ability to effectively communicate. It's important that we not just participate in frequent conversation, but we must master the art of effective communication. What do we mean by that? If we are speaking English, but our spouse's only language is French. The words coming out are not the issue. The ability to understand, translate and respond to those words will be of great concern. We must evaluate and continue to sharpen our communication styles to appeal to the needs of our spouse. This will go a long way in not only preserving peace, but it shows our spouse that we respect their needs. Sometimes, in marriage, we must esteem our spouses needs above our own. Philippians 2:3 says, *"Do nothing out of selfish ambition or vain conceit. Rather, in humility value others above yourselves."* Just as helpful as it is to evaluate our various personality traits, it would do us as much good to analyze our communication styles. Here's a brief description of the 5 commonly used styles. Let's see if we find a bit of ourselves or our spouses in these descriptions, provided to us by *psychology.com:*

Aggressive Communication style

- This type of style can focus on winning even if it is on the other person's expense. They behave as if their needs are more important, have more to contribute, and have more rights than other people. This is not a healthy style of communication because the content of the message can be lost because people become too busy reacting to the way it is delivered.

- They are frightening, threatening and hostile. They are out to win and the use different methods such as bullying, intimidation, abrasiveness, demanding, unpredictability, and belligerence. They volume is loud and the posture is bigger than others. They invade other people's spaces and try to stand over them. Their facial expressions can be glaring, frowning, and scowling. The other person is likely to feel defensive, hurt, humiliated, resentful, afraid, and ultimately does not respect the other person.

The Passive-Aggressive Communication Style

- This is a communication style where a person appears to be passive on the outside, but are indirectly acting out their anger. People employing this style of communication usually feel powerless, and undermine the object of their resentments subtly to express how they feel, even if it means sabotaging themselves. A good expression that can be used to describe them is "cutting off your nose to spite your face"

- They are indirectly aggressive and sarcastic. They are not reliable and can be dubious, sulky, gossips, patronizing, and complainers. Their expressions are inconsistent with their true feelings and will be pleasant to your face but poisonous behind your back. They have a sugary sweet voice and an asymmetrical posture. They have a sweet and innocent facial expression. People on the receiving end will feel confused, resentful, angry, and hurt.

The Submissive Communication Style

- This type of person will try his/her best to please others and avoid conflict. They treat the needs of other as more important than theirs. They behave as if the other person has more rights and more to contribute. They are apologetic because they feel as if they are imposing when they want something. They try their best to avoid any confrontation and will yield to preferences of other people. They feel like the victim and they refuse compliments. They don't express their desires or how they are feeling.

- They use a soft volume and try to make themselves as small as possible. They tend to fidget a lot and will portray submissive behaviors. People on the receiving end will feel guilty, frustrated, exasperated, and don't know what they want.

The Manipulative Communication Style

- People employing this style are scheming, shrewd and calculating. Manipulative communicators are great at influencing and controlling others for their own benefit. They have an underlying message when they speak, and many times the other person is unaware. They are cunning, control other people in an insidious way such as sulking, using fake tears, indirectly asking for their needs to be met, and making the other person feel sorry or obliged to help them.

- They can have a patronizing, ingratiating, envious, and often high pitched voice. The other person will be left feeling guilty, angry, frustrated, irritated, and not sure of where to stand with them.

We are separate, but equal. There are many traits that make us different from our spouses. Remember we are all made in the perfect image and likeness of God. Our composition (mental, physical and emotional) are all intentional and necessary attributes that work together to make us who we are. Our goals should not be to change who we are. Instead, we should work to always improve yourself. Likewise, we should never work to change our spouses. Our focus should be improving how we live, work and communicate them. This process of loving, accepting and growing in wisdom and maturity with each other, will help make us champions, both in life and in marriage.

CHAMPIONS IN MARRIAGE
Questions & Discussion
Chapter 11: Personality Differences

1. How would you describe your personality?

2. How are you different from your spouse?

3. In what ways are your differences a compliment to each other?

_____

_____

_____

_____

_____

_____

_____

_____

_____

CHAPTER 12
I Change My Mind
**What Happens If Your Spouse Changes
Sexuality, Identity or Preferences?**

In the beginning, we are most likely dating a representative. In the hilarious stand up comedy routine, Chris Rock: Bigger and Blacker, comedian Chris Rock performed a racy, yet hilarious set around the complexities of relationships. One of the most memorable lines he said in his 1999 blockbuster show is, "When you meet someone for the first time, you're not meeting them, you're meeting their representative." How funny and true is that statement? When we are preparing for that first date, most of us don't pull out whatever outfit is in our every 4-day rotation, we pick out the best of what we have to offer. Sometimes that may mean making an all new purchase. But it doesn't just stop at our attire, does it? The razors are coming out, we are shaving, putting on new fragrances and spending extra time with our hair. We arrive to our location with an extra pep in our step and smile on our face. We are full of personality and just the ideal picture of a good time. If the date goes well, we may keep that facade up for days, weeks and even months. Ultimately, little-by-little guards start coming down. Once we know we've got this relationship in the bag, without even intending to, we start back acting more like our true selves. We get mad at the things that make us angry. We don't laugh at the things we don't think are funny. We wear what is comfortable, rather than what is cute. Some people switch from their representative to their authentic self immediately, for others it happens over time. The version of the person we end up with may be completely different from the one we dated.

We have to reconcile our checklist with reality. Subconsciously, most of us have a checklist before entering into marriage. Some lists are more extensive than others, but for the most part, we have some criteria of what we were looking for in a potential mate. Perhaps, a certain race, religion or height. Maybe a preference of them having or not having children, being a dog lover, or enjoying a certain pastime. In our minds, our checklist is there to help us choose a mate that will be most compatible and to our liking. It's laughable how far some of us veer from our original checklist once love kicks in. The fact is, in most cases, it's opposites that attract. What we originally find alluring, later becomes annoying. When the dust settles and time passes, we will all have to sit down and reconcile the differences between our checklists and our realities. Some of us marry a person based on what we feel is their potential. Their potential was on our checklist. Despite potential, reality dictates that our spouse may not be the person we thought. If and when that day comes, we will have to take a long hard look at ourselves. Once we make our vows, everything in our relationships should be negotiable. Our perceived reality and our spouses' true identity have a way of catching up to one another.

Whether a mid-life crisis or full blown identity crisis, at some point, couples question what they want. As we grow older and wiser, our tolerances and preferences may change. At age 10, if someone asked us what we wanted for lunch, our answer might be peanut butter and jelly. If they asked us that same question now, there is a plethora of answers we might offer. Why? Our palette has grown and our experiences have matured. Our favorite television shows to watch 20 years ago is likely to be different than our favorite shows today. It's not that we don't still like the old things, we evolve.

Why is it so inconceivable when we find it happening in our relationships? Our spouses or our marriages is subject to change. When we realize that we or our spouse are becoming a different person, it's important that we not necessarily panic. In fact, we would be wise to expect some changes, because change is a sign of growth. The key is to keep the lines of communication open so that changes are being experienced together, rather than one person feeling like it happened overnight.

Don't let your spouse's identity crisis make you question *your identity.* Some couples will face extreme versions of identity crisis. It may be hard to imagine, but many more couples are finding ourselves having conversations that we never imagined, like finding out our spouse is gay, lesbian or feeling trapped in the wrong body gender. For those of us who, God-forbid, ever find ourselves having to tackle this complex issue, we are not alone. There is an organization called "The Straight Spouse Network," founded to support spouses who find themselves in a marriage with a spouse who changes sexual orientation. They published a study in November 2018 on couples who find themselves in this devastating predicament. According to the Straight Spouse Network there is an estimated 2 million mixed orientation couples. Furthermore, this study showed that when the gay, lesbian, or bisexual partner comes out, a third of the couples break up immediately; another third stay together for one to two years and then split; the remaining third try to make their marriages work. Of these, half split up, while the other half stay together for three or more years. Similarly, The Family Pride Coalition also released a compiled report of the following statistics:

- 20 percent of all gay men in America are in a heterosexual marriage.

- 50 percent of all gay men in America have fathered children.
- 40 percent of all lesbians in America are married to a male partner.
- 75 percent of all lesbians have children.

Avoid the tendency to try to change or convert them back to the spouse you once knew. Regardless of the extremity of our spouse's apparent personality or identity change, we must resist the urge to try to personally and single-handedly change them. God made us all free-will agents. Even with the generous sacrifice of his only son for our salvation, He never tries to force himself on us. He gives us the choice of life and death, heaven and hell. If He doesn't try to manipulate or coerce his way on us, we shouldn't deploy those tactics on our spouse. No matter how minor or severe our displeasure is with our spouses' choice and lifestyle, we must resist the urge to manipulate or guilt them into seeing things our way. Some issues require thorough communication and behavior modification. Other issues require counseling and mediation. These complexities can only be solved by fasting and prayer. God has a way of fixing our spouses a lot faster and more effectively than we ever could. Some changes in preference or identity are to be expected and worked through. Others are much more severe and require an entirely higher level of intervention, counseling and Holy Spirit-led decision-making. Whatever the ultimate course of action or outcome, it will not be easy, but God is able to make all grace abound toward us, exactly when we need it most.

Extend grace and forgiveness regardless of the situation. We can find every self-help book imaginable and read the Bible from cover to cover and find no sense of relief. There may not be a single chapter more helpful and insightful in these cases than Matthew chapter 5. This chapter teaches us how to deal with others who have wronged us and God's position on divorce. Rather than listing 40 plus verses, let's challenge ourselves to read it on our own, with open hearts, minds and spirits. God is capable of giving more revelation and personal instruction in those verses than we could ever offer. Many of the scriptures will be debatable and open to an array of public opinions. What is universally agreed upon is the plea to treat others in a spirit of love, grace and forgiveness. The standard of character and challenge of goodness in this chapter will be irrefutable. Although difficult to adhere to at times, with Christ as our perfect example, let us examine ourselves, our lives and our situations through the lenses of these verses (see Mathew 5:1-48).

CHAMPIONS IN MARRIAGE
Questions & Discussion
Chapter 12: I Change My Mind

1. In what ways have you grown or evolved since you first met your spouse?

2. What changes have you noticed in your partner, since that time?

3. How can you ensure that you are keeping your spouse "up to date" of where you are, and who you are becoming?

_____

_____

_____

_____

_____

_____

_____

_____

CHAPTER 13
OVERCOMING LOSS
Repossession and Foreclosure

Houston, we have a problem. In 1995, director Ron Howard released the American space docudrama film, Apollo 13, starring Tom Hanks, Kevin Bacon, Bill Paxton, Gary Sinise, and Ed Harris. This film depicted the brave and heroic astronauts aboard Apollo 13 for America's third mission to land on the moon. The phrase "Houston, we have a problem" was dramatically used and perpetuated as the universal line that indicates that amidst, an otherwise pleasant and ordinary experience, we have now hit a snag. In marriage, sometimes we hit snags. Things can be going fairly well. Money flowing. Children behaving. Our relationship is in a good place and we're feeling grateful and maybe even blissful. Then out of nowhere, life happens. Something completely unexpected comes along and blindsides us and nearly wipes us out. For many marriages in America, nothing derails our train and sinks our ships like the loss of income, finance and worldly possessions.

Financial stress weighs significantly on a marriage. During premarital counseling finances are described as one of the leading causes of divorce. It turns out, even to this day, there's statistical evidence to back that statement. A recent study, conducted by Experian (Consumer Credit Service) revealed that of the 50 percent of all marriages that end in divorce, 59 percent of divorcees surveyed say that finances played at least "somewhat" of a role in their divorces, while 20 percent believe it played a "big" role. Additionally, 36 percent say their spouse's credit score was a huge source of stress in their marriage. Unfortunately, many of us are simply not aware of the many resources available that can help us better manage our finances. By the time we do, in most cases it's too late. That's why at the first sign of a problem, we have to put pride aside and do everything we can to seek the right assistance. For our marriage, this could literally be a life or death decision.

We must accept our finances, and then address it. Many of us are in a financial boat with a leak in it. We see that we are losing income and piling up bills, but feel helpless in knowing what steps to take. The single worst thing we can do is stand on the sidelines and do nothing. The moment we see we have a financial hemorrhage, of any kind, we must take the proper precautions to stop, acknowledge and admit we are drowning. Professionals at *bankrate.com* offer married couples a few practical pointers on where to start getting a handle on debt. In an article entitled "6 Tips to Manage Debt and Save Your Marriage", financially distressed couples are advised to:

1. Have an Honest Discussion about Debt

You would be surprised how many financial secrets are often kept between husband and wife. Some spouses may spend more money on a monthly basis than the other realizes. Other spouses may have carried over large (secret) debts that they are trying to manage in an effort to avoid the other's knowledge and judgment. Steve Repak, a financial planning professional, financial literacy speaker and author says, "Sunlight is the best disinfectant, so one of the best 1st steps is to share with each other how much you owe and the interest rate on each of the debts." Even if only one spouse is responsible for the accumulated debt, the key to preserving our marriage will be committing to work together to pay it off.

2. Prioritize our Debts

The concept of truly prioritizing our debts, must not only be comprehended in theory, but adhered to in reality. "Always pay for necessities first: food, clothing and shelter," says Kevin Gallegos, vice president of sales and Phoenix operations for Freedom Financial Network. "That means the basics — not dining out, new wardrobes and a mini-mansion," he says. As an additional word of advice, Gallegos also suggests that in putting necessities at the top of our list, we have to be sure to pay at least the minimum on any of our secured debt, or loans that are secured by a tangible asset such as a car or a home. He advises, "If you do not pay these bills on time, you could lose the asset, which in the case of a car or home can cause major life problems."

3. Create a Debt Payoff Plan

After evaluating the debt together, couples should then work as partners to come up with the best method of payoff for our households. There are several methods of debt management, we just have to choose which one works best for us. According to *bankrate.com*, two such methods are considered to be the Avalanche Method and the Snowball Method. With the avalanche method, we start paying off the debt with the highest interest rate and work down, making minimum payments on each debt except the one with the highest rate for which we pay any extra we can afford until it's paid off. Then we are advised to continue paying the same monthly total, but put the extra toward the debt with the next highest interest rate, and so on. Another option is the snowball method, in which we could pay off the smallest debt amount first and work up from there. Each month, we are encouraged to pay the minimum on all debts and apply any remaining funds toward paying off the debt with the smallest balance. When that debt is paid, we should continue paying the same monthly amount we started with, applying extra funds toward our second-smallest debt, and so on.

4. Change our Mindset

If there is a spouse that tends to be a bigger spender, shopping habits will need to be curtailed, for as long as it takes. We will not just have to change our spending habits, we will have to change our entire mindset, for lasting change. "If you pay off debt only to charge up the credit cards or sign for a new car loan a few weeks or months later, you will have ultimately gained nothing," Gallegos says. Even if we're focused on investing money in stocks or other investments, it may be time to suspend those spending habits temporarily. Again, many credit many experts agree that "few investments can top the rate of return for eliminating debt", furthermore "Paying off credit card debt at typical interest rates effectively makes an investment that returns 15% to 20% or more per year", Gallegos cites.

5. Negotiate as Needed

When at all possible, it's best for us to self-manage the consoli-

-dation of our debts. Nonetheless, there are occasions when, due to lack of available time or personal expertise, it's best to consult a professional. There's nothing wrong with seeking outside financial assistance. In fact, sometimes, it is what's best. Experts commonly advise that as we work to pay down our debts, we can often call creditors and ask for temporary hardship status, if we feel we may qualify. Many lenders and financial institutions would prefer a negotiated pay of our debt, rather than a potential total debt cancellation. So, reaching out to negotiate terms and options can, at times, be a win-win for all parties.

6. Develop a Plan for Future Spending

When financial disaster strikes, we may find ourselves going into crisis management mode and developing a strict budget. It is important, however, in setting realistic, long term goals, that we give ourselves enough wiggle room to breathe and plan for the unexpected. If our budgets are so tight that we don't even allot for an impromptu cup of coffee, we may be setting ourselves up for a form of future stress that's even greater than our current situation. Dr. Taffi Wilkens Wagner, owner of Money Talks LLC says, "To avoid feeling trapped, determine an amount of money you can each spend, without consulting your partner."

She continues by adding, "The idea is *not* to create more financial stress and strain, yet alleviate what is causing unhappy times in the marriage." Instead, Wagner recommends that as spouses, we each agree to make purchases in cash or with a debit card rather than using credit cards. She suggests that when we have to pay cash, it may often be easier to determine whether the purchase is a need or a want. The goal for long-term planning, again, is to not make us feel we are in prison, but with the right financial mediation and spending moderation, we should be able to establish new financial plans that actually liberate us from debt-stress, and set us on a path toward a financially healthier marriage.

If the worst happens, and we suffer repossession, foreclosure or bankruptcy, we must find a way to keep it together, and stick together. There's no more gut-wrenching a feeling than working as hard as you can, cutting spending, saving money, negotiating with creditors, all to no avail. Losing the very thing you were fighting to hold on to is a challenging crisis that requires mutual support. Repossession, foreclosure and bankruptcy can happen to the best of us – even the brightest, smartest and the richest. According to the United States Courts, over the last 5 years, the number of people who file for bankruptcy every year have ranged between 800,000 and 1,000,083. These cases were not *all* due to extravagant spending or negligent fiscal planning. Sometimes couples fall victim of a life-altering health crisis or traumatic event that racks up more bills than income. Other times there could be a shift in our economy, government or field of work that causes layoffs, corporate shutdowns and job downsizing. For any number of reasons, repossession, foreclosure and bankruptcy are each devastating occurrences that wreak absolute havoc on our marriages. In the midst of adversities, we must remember to be intentional about holding it together emotionally and psychologically. We must also cleave closer together in our marriages and for our families. Major financial losses are a prime reason to fault-find and finger-point. The truth is, in these exasperating times, we need each other more than ever. Couples who are able to hold on through traumatic occurrences like this, will almost always re-emerge stronger. Sure, it's initially embarrassing to explain why we are no longer driving the car or living in the house we used to own. However, temporary and external embarrassment doesn't compare to the potential long-lasting, internal devastation felt after divorce. We may lose our possessions, maybe even a few friends, but let's determine in our minds that we won't lose our marriage. We can overcome any loss – couples do it everyday. At the end of the day, our marriage and family is our most valuable asset.

CHAMPIONS IN MARRIAGE
Questions & Discussion
Chapter 13: Overcoming Loss

1. Up to this point, what has been your most costly financial loss or mistake?

2. How did you rebound?

3. What steps can you take to safeguard your financial future?

_____

_____

_____

_____

_____

_____

_____

_____

_____

_____

CHAPTER 14
Dealing with Death:
How to Keep Grief from Killing the Marriage

Death alters our lives every bit as much as birth does. When a firstborn infant enters a family, the presence of that new life is awe-inspiring. This life-altering event is miraculous and changes everything, from our sleep and work hours to routine activities. Our cost of living and budgets remain forever changed. Places we used to go without a moment's notice now take careful planning and forethought. Many mothers can testify that even their body composition and shape is forever changed. Dads also view the world from a more mature perspective. The entrance of a new life changes everything. The only thing that compare to the gravity of birth is death. Death is the permanent cessation of life. Unlike separation or divorce, it is permanent and completely irreversible.

Death may yield a complex process of grief. Whether it is the death of a parent, close friend or family member, death affects couples in completely unpredictable ways. God forbid having to cope with the reality of losing a child, some people withdraw – others act out negatively. There are those spouses that feel unusually clingy. Unfortunately, some stop communicating all together. The key to getting through this complex and unforeseen circumstance is allowing each spouse to grieve according to their needs. *Pat Schwiebert, R.N. is t*he founder and creative director of Grief Watch. She is also the author of many books, including *Tear Soup, a recipe for healing after loss, We We're Gonna Have a Baby... But Had an Angel Instead, and When Hello Means Goodbye.* She has also created a number of other resources to help people through the grieving process. According to Schwiebert, there are 5 major dangers signs to watch for when it comes to grieving in a marriage:

1. **Be aware of any tendency to want to inflict on to your partner the hurt that you are feeling.**

Because we are different people with two different sets of past experiences and perspectives, it is only natural to expect there to be some variance in our actions and reactions. Furthermore, we must resist the urge to make our spouse feel like they have to cry, if we cry. Differences in reaction don't mean that one spouse cares any more, or less, there may just be variances in how we process grief.

2. **Don't expect your partner to be your sole source of emotional support.**

Death can take a mental, emotional and sometimes physical toll on us. We need outlets, and plenty of them. Because we may each be grieving in our own way, it's important that we not over-extend ourselves to each other or have unrealistic expectations of our capabilities during such a vulnerable time.

3. Keep a list of names and phone numbers of other persons that you can call on short notice.

When we feel the walls caving in on us, and grief is enveloping us like a blanket, it would be helpful to have a few lifelines on speed dial, to offer that word of advice or way of escape.

4. When you and your partner can't talk with each other because the pain is too great, write notes to each other.

There's nothing like writing a good old-fashioned love note to make our loved one feel special. It's a great reminder, in an otherwise tough time, that we are not alone. Writing a note also says that even in the midst of our worst pain, our hearts and minds are still on each other.

5. Look for ways that you can please your partner or at least ease some of your partner's pain.

It doesn't always take big, grand gestures to put a smile on a person's face. We may not show up with a dozen roses or bouquet of balloons, but everyday we can at least do one small, simple thing to show our spouse that we care. Perhaps, we bring home our spouse's favorite candy or snack. Maybe we take on a chore that will normally be done by our partner. Whatever it is, like the old saying goes, "What comes from the heart, reaches the heart".

In our quest to identify helpful resources for those dealing with death and loss, we came across *familyfriendpoems.com*, a wonderful outlet for everyday poets to express love & healing. Page 120 in this book highlights a sample of the beautiful poetry about grief titled, *Basket of Burdens.* It beautifully expresses the pain and hope of anyone who is grieving the loss of a loved one. May God grant you comfort and peace.

THIS BASKET OF BURDENS
© Debbie
Published March 2010

My Basket of burdens
Is filled with the grief of my loss
It is so heavy to carry
Although this road I must cross.

This pathway through life
Feels unbearable at times
And I don't have the strength
For this mountain I climb.

The Basket's filled with sorrow
Oh, how I miss my love
At first, it's impossible to carry,
Where is my help from above?

It's draining my strength
I can't do anymore
This pain goes so deep
Right down to my core.

As I carry this Basket
I'll learn to manage the weight
Each step of the way
Will become easier they say.

But how do they know,
Have they been here before?
If so, where's their Basket
They're responsible for?

This Basket of burdens
You can't see and can't touch
I carry it inside me
This pain is too much.

Patience is needed to carry
This loss that I feel
A shoulder to lean on
So, someday I will heal.

God sent my family
My friends and spirits unknown
So, I won't carry this Basket
Forever alone

Someday, I'll lay down my Basket
With burdens' no more
My pain will be gone
When, I cross through that door

CHAMPIONS IN MARRIAGE
Questions & Discussion
Chapter 14: Dealing with Death

1. Who is the "closest" person your heart that you've lost by death?

2. What was the initial impact of that death?

3. How does that loss currently affect your life?

_____

_____

_____

_____

_____

_____

_____

_____

_____

NOTES TO PAGES

1. Saul Levine, MD, Professor Emeritus in Psychiatry University of California at San Diego (UCSD) slevine@ucsd.edu https://www.psychologytoday.com/us/blog/our-emotional-footprint/201512/the-denial-reality / p. 20
2. Carl Alaska, MD "How Does Denial Work: https://www.psychologytoday.com/us/blog/beyond-blame/201204/how-does-denial-actually-work / p.20
3. American Psychological Association (Divorce Rates) https://www.apa.org/topics/divorce/ / p. 18
4. Forgiveness: Letting go of Grudges and Bitterness. Mayo Clinic https://www.mayoclinic.org/healthy-lifestyle/adult-health/in-depth/forgiveness/art-20047692 / p. 22
5. Focus on the Family (Divorce Rates amongst Christians) (CORE COMMONALITIES) https://www.focusonthefamily.com/about/focus-findings/marriage/divorce-rate-in-the-church-as-high-as-the-world / p. 65
6. The Holy Bible / References based on KJV/ NIV / Message / Message Versions
7. Infertility- https://resolve.org/infertility-101/what-is-infertility/fast-facts/ / p. 37
8. A Miracle of Conception- http://www.tribune242.com/news/2015/aug/04/miracle-conception// p. 38
9. High Divorce Rate of Second and Third Marriages: https://www.psychologytoday.com/us/blog/the-intelligent divorce/201202/the-high-failure-rate-second-and-third-marriages / p. 45-46
10. Intimacy- https://www.psychologytoday.com/us/blog/romantically-attached/201802/the-7-elements-define-intimate-relationship / p. 51
11. Sex- https://www.familylife.com/articles/topics/life-issues/challenges/homosexuality/why-did-god-invent-sex// p. 52-26
12. Women Carry DNA of ALL Sexual Partners https://gnosticwarrior.com/women-may-carry-the-dna-of-all-their-sexual-partners.html / p. 52
13. Divorce Rates/Church Attendance- https://www.focusonthefamily.com/about/focus-findings/marriage/divorce-rate-in-the-church-as-high-as-the-world / p. 65
14. Sickness & Divorce- https://www.medicaldaily.com/sickness-and-health-marriages-are-more-likely-end-divorce-if-wife-gets-sick-324776 / p. 84

NOTES TO PAGES continued...

15. Enduring Love Stories- https://www.myasd.com/blog/7-enduring-love-stories-death-could-not-separate / p. 85-86
16. Chris Rock: Bigger & Blacker: https://www.youtube.com/watch?v=441c3FKWYJo / p.116
17. Gay, Lesbian Spouse- http://www.straightspouse.org/who-we-are/history/ https://www.verywellmind.com/if-your-spouse-is-gay-2300962 / p. 119
18. Personality Test- https://www.myersbriggs.org/myers-and-briggs-foundation// p. 107
19. Communication Styles- https://dspsychology.com.au/5-styles-of-communication/ p. 109-112
20. Financial Stress- https://www.prnewswire.com/news-releases/how-much-of-a-role-do-finances-play-in-divorce-300405756.html / p. 124
21. Getting Control of Debt- https://www.bankrate.com/finance/debt/manage-debt-and-marriage-1.aspx#slide=4 / p. 125
22. Bankruptcy- https://www.uscourts.gov/news/2018/07/24/june-2018-bankruptcy-filings-fall-26-percent / p. 126-130
23. Death Poem- https://www.familyfriendpoems.com/poem/this-basket-of-burdens / 138

www.ingramcontent.com/pod-product-compliance
Lightning Source LLC
LaVergne TN
LVHW051245080426
835513LV00016B/1742